FAITH

— *of* —

OUR FATHERS

FAITH
—of—
OUR FATHERS

Under the Microscope of Reason and History

> For Rekha and Suresh

" To understand just one life, you have
to swallow the world". p. 121
Midnight's Children" by Salmon Rushdie

> Best Wishes. Ron Evans
July, 2013

RONALD V. EVANS

iUniverse, Inc.
Bloomington

Faith of Our Fathers
Under the Microscope of Reason and History

iUniverse books may be ordered through booksellers or by contacting:

iUniverse
1663 Liberty Drive
Bloomington, IN 47403
www.iuniverse.com
1-800-Authors (1-800-288-4677)

ISBN: 978-1-4759-9383-7 (sc)
ISBN: 978-1-4759-9384-4 (ebk)

Library of Congress Control Number: 2013909956

Printed in the United States of America

iUniverse rev. date: 06/20/2013

CONTENTS

To my Great Grandchildren.
Emma, Kristen and Alex.

Acknowledgements

I am grateful for the encouragement and support of family and friends in writing this book. I particularly wish to thank my wife Lois, my partner in life and closest friend.

To those of you who have read and edited my manuscript, I offer my sincere thanks. Thank you, also, for your suggestions and insights.

- Sandra Beaulieu
- Dorothy and Geoff Coates
- Bill and Randi Evans
- Paul Blake
- Janine Towle (also my second draft reader)
- Rhonda Milligan
- Linda D'Amico
- Kathleen Sowerby
- Bill Sowerby (cover design)

The four cover images are used with the courtesy of:

1. Kirsty Pargeter-Fotolia.com
2. Floki Fotos-Fotolia.com
3. Arturaliev-Fotolia.com
4. NASA, ESA, and The Hubble Heritage Team STScl/AURA)

INTRODUCTION

Before I put the "Faith of Our Fathers"[1] under the microscope, I would like to explain why I wrote this book and, in doing so, give you my background. Primarily, I wrote this book for people who have "lost it". In spite of loving parents who saw them baptized and confirmed, and who took them to church, they have lost the faith they once held. Perhaps they were disillusioned by the hypocritical behaviour of professing Christians, including the scandalous behaviour of priests and evangelists. Perhaps they gave up on the Bible because they found it to be archaic and irrelevant. Perhaps their exposure to modern science undermined the faith they once held in miracles, the efficacy of prayer, heaven, and hell. Perhaps they looked at the chaos and suffering in the world with its diseases, wars, genocides, earthquakes, and floods, and concluded that there was no one in charge—no omnipotent, compassionate God with a divine plan. Whatever their reasons, they have "lost it".

I also had in mind Christians who are troubled by their doubts and questions. For years they were passive listeners or readers, but not anymore. There was a time when they believed scripture was relevant to today's issues. Now, they are not so sure. Some worry about their skepticism. Are they in the right to criticize and question what they have been taught?

Lastly, I wrote this book for conservative Christians who accept the Bible as literally true and historically accurate—the inerrant Word of God. I doubt that many conservative Christians will consider what I see under my microscope. A pity. They could gain new insights if they reflected on

---

[1]   These are the first four words of a hymn written by Frederick William Faber (1814-1863).

the topics listed in the content page; e.g., the authors of the gospels, the nativity stories, creationism versus evolution, and the Book of Genesis.

I can identify with each of these groups. I was raised in a Christian home with loving parents who practised the Golden Rule of doing unto others, as you would have done unto you. I went to church every Sunday. I was a member of the choir and Young Peoples. I even taught Sunday School. When I was 16, I read the Gospel According to St. John, and accepted Jesus Christ as my Lord and Saviour. In high school I joined the Varsity Christian Fellowship. I believed in the Bible as God's answer to all our questions and problems.

I did more than accept the "Faith of Our Fathers." I decided to become a minister. One of my friends made the same decision, opting to attend the Moody Bible Institute in Chicago. I wavered between attending Moody or the University of Toronto. My conservative friends advised me not to attend a secular university. They said my faith would be undermined because I would be taught by atheists and agnostics. I decided that if my faith was worth holding, it would stand the test of a university education. I enrolled at Victoria College of the University of Toronto.

My friends were wrong about my teachers. Many were active members of mainstream Christian churches. In fact, one of my history teachers was an Anglican priest. But they were right about Professor Staples, who taught me Near Eastern History. He did challenge my faith. Knowing that some of us were headed for the ministry, he delighted in shocking us. I can picture him now, peering over the top of his glasses to see if he had got our attention by one of his tidbits of Sumerian history. He pointed out, to my amazement, that the Babylonians had their own story of Noah and the Ark. In another lecture he discounted the originality of the Genesis story of Adam and Eve, and the serpent in the Garden of Eden.[2]

When I entered university I had never heard of carbon dating—a scientific technique[3] for determining the age of ancient artifacts such as

---

[2]   The Genesis account was based on an earlier Sumerian story, preserved on a clay tablet—carbon dated to c.3500 BCE. Sumer was an ancient civilization in southern Mesopotamia (modern Iraq). This story has a serpent, a tree, and a goddess who gives the fruit of life to a visiting male. See Campbell, Joseph. *The Power of Myth: with Bill Moyers.* New York: Doubleday, a division of Bantam Doubleday Dell Publishing Group, Inc., 1988, 54.

[3]   See Addendum F, Geological Clocks.

bones, wooden tools, clothing, and papyrus. Nor had I read the works of Thomas Hobbes, Emmanuel Kant, Jean-Jacques Rousseau, Soren Kierkegaard, Karl Marx, or Albert Einstein. I was only vaguely aware of the accomplishments of scientists like Copernicus, Galileo, Charles Darwin, or Albert Einstein. I was only 18, but naively confident I could answer the big four religious questions: Who am I? Where did I come from? Why am I here? Where am I going?

As a prerequisite for the ministry, I studied Hebrew. By the end of my second year, I was able to read all the chapters in the Book of Genesis. As I translated the various chapters, I noticed various styles of writing with marked differences in vocabulary and sentence structure. It was obvious that no one person could have written Genesis. It was a compilation of different authors and stories. But I had been taught that the first five books of the Bible, the Torah, had been written by Moses. That is exactly what my edition of the Bible stated in the title pages of Genesis, Exodus, Leviticus, Numbers and Deuteronomy. For me it was a disturbing paradox. Who and why would anyone tamper with God's Word?

In my second and third years I studied Greek, another prerequisite for theology at Emmanuel College. It was one of my best subjects, thanks to my four years of high school Latin. In my last semester, I could translate chapters from the gospels and the epistles. Four semesters of Greek did not make me a New Testament expert, but at least I could appreciate the scholarship necessary in translating Greek into English—particularly if you had to choose from a dozen varying Greek manuscripts.

In spite of my growing list of religious questions, I began my first year of theology with optimism. Emmanuel College had an enviable, scholarly reputation, due in part to its close affiliation with Victoria University and the University of Toronto. All my professors held doctoral degrees. I was confident they would help me find answers to my nagging doubts, accumulated over three years of undergraduate study.

I was mistaken. Three years later, I found myself standing alone in the foyer of the college. I had just written my last exam. In two weeks I would be ordained. With my wife Lois and our newborn daughter, Sandra, I was soon to leave for a pastoral charge at Nobel, just north of Parry Sound, Ontario. Yet, there I stood full of anxiety, wondering if I should go through with my ordination. I thought remorsefully of the thousands of dollars it had cost my denomination to subsidize my theological education. I wondered what my parents and friends would think. I thought guiltily about my home congregation. They had been so proud and supportive of me, their first ministerial candidate. What would they think?

I resolved my dilemma by deciding to stay in the ministry for five years. I would use my summer vacation time to take courses in Clinical Pastoral training, offered through McMaster University. I determined to be the best pastor I could be, but I also promised myself that I would leave the ministry in five years time, if I still felt the same as I did standing there in the foyer of Emmanuel College.

After five years in the ministry, I made my decision. It was really a no-brainer for a number of reasons. Preparing the sermons and prayers had become an agonizing chore, taking up to 20 hours a week to prepare. I analyzed and questioned everything I wrote. All too often I completed my Sunday sermon late on Saturday night. My wife, Lois, was not amused. It also took an inordinate amount of time for me to choose prayers for church or funeral services. I found much of the language in the Book of Common Order to be archaic, exaggerated forms of servile flattery.

> *O God, the Protector of all that trust in Thee, without whom nothing is strong, nothing is holy . . . O Lord our heavenly Father, high and mighty, King of Kings, Lord of Lords, the only Ruler of princes, who dost from thy throne behold all the dwellers upon earth . . . Eternal and ever blessed God, we bow before thy Divine Majesty.*

I felt certain that an intelligent, caring Creator would gag at such adulation. This objection carried over to some of the hymns. One Sunday morning the congregation rose to sing this opening verse of praise.

> *Holy, Holy, Holy, Lord God Almighty.*
> *Early in the morning our songs shall rise to Thee.*
> *Holy, Holy, Holy, Merciful and Mighty,*
> *God in Three Persons, Blessed Trinity.*

I was jarred by a disturbing thought. Did God want to be called "Holy" not once, but six times in one verse? Suddenly, the words I had sung so often seemed absurd. Why would an intelligent, benevolent deity want or need to be incessantly praised and adored? It was instantly clear to me why I had become very selective in the hymns I chose. I disliked those that were repetitive in their regal praise of God. I steered clear of those that had us grovelling on our knees as miserable sinners. I avoided hymns portraying God as a deity appeased by the blood of His Son. As you can appreciate, my choice of hymns was rather limited.

It was obvious that I could no longer, in good conscience, remain in the ministry. In May I submitted my resignation. By July I was again a student enrolled at the Ontario College of Education in Toronto, and by September I was teaching English at Central Secondary School in Hamilton, Ontario. With my counselling background, I was given a half-timetable of Guidance. Five years later I was Head of a Counselling Department. It was a rewarding and challenging career for the next 28 years, until I retired.

Thus, I left the ministry but, ironically, I remained an avid reader of theology and church history. I followed with interest the remarkable discoveries of early Egyptian manuscripts—52 ancient scrolls near Nag Hammadi in 1945[4], the Dead Sea Scrolls in 1947 in caves near the Dead Sea, and the Gospel of Judas Iscariot found in the late 1970's. I read many of the "lost" Christian texts such as the *Didache*, the (Infancy) *Gospel of Thomas*, the Coptic *Gospel of Thomas*, the *Secret Gospel of Mark*, and the *Shepherd of Hermas*.

Four years ago I began organizing my notes and writing "*Faith of Our Fathers*" *Under the Microscope of Reason and History*. In the bibliography I have listed my major resource books. For the chapters dealing with the geological clocks of science, I am indebted to Dr. Geoffrey Coates who has a background in physics and nuclear medicine, and my brother, William Evans, with his background as a high school science teacher.

I invite you to look with me at the "faith of our fathers" through the microscope of reason and history. As you do so, you will be examining your own faith. Although there is a planned order to the sequencing of the chapters, some may prefer to use the Table of Contents as their guide to topics of particular interest.

---

[4]   Access to the scrolls was limited initially to Jewish scholars. The first English translations came out in 1962. Scholarly reviews from European and North American theologians were published in the 1980's and 1990's.

CHAPTER 1

Who Wrote the New Testament Gospels?[5]

For centuries Christians have been taught that the four New Testament gospels were historical biographies recorded by the first disciples of Jesus—eyewitnesses! I, too, assumed the New Testament gospels were written by the first disciples. It is a logical assumption because these gospels are entitled with the names of the early disciples—According to Matthew, Mark, Luke, and John. To my surprise, in my first year of theology, I learned from my course in textual analysis that the four gospels were written in Greek, decades after the death of Jesus—and not by any of the first 12 disciples.

Somehow I had missed the obvious fact that each gospel is written in the third person—hardly the style of an eyewitness. Nor had I given much thought as to how ordinary, illiterate disciples, whose daily language was Aramaic, became proficient in Greek prose! The writer of Acts 4:13 had no such illusions. *Now when they saw the boldness of Peter and John, and perceived that they were uneducated, common men, they wondered . . .*

If any New Testament figure could have written a biography about Jesus, it would have been the Apostle Paul. We know from his epistles that he began his ministry shortly after the crucifixion and that he

---

5   By the third century there were over 20 gospels, all claiming to have been written by prominent early Christians: e.g. *the Gospel of Paul, the Gospel of Bartholomew,* and *the Gospel of Mary Magdalene.*

1

died, according to Christian tradition, circa (c.) 64 of the Christian Era (CE), martyred during the reign of Emperor Nero. Although he was a contemporary of Jesus, he never joined the multitudes to see and hear Jesus of Nazareth.

Paul, who wrote in the decades immediately following the life of Jesus, gives us no personal information about Jesus' childhood, his adolescence, his physical features, or his family. Nor does he mention the Virgin Birth, the nativity stories, Pontius Pilate, Mary Magdalene, Judas Iscariot, the raising of Lazarus from the dead, the Golden Rule, the parables of Jesus, the Lord's Prayer, or the Sermon on the Mount. Are these not remarkable omissions?

In his epistles to the first Christian communities, Paul never mentions the Gospels According to Matthew, Mark, Luke, or John. There is a good reason. When Paul preached, these gospels had not yet been written. As we will see in chapter seven, "Early Christian Authors (100 to 400)," in the debates of the second century, early Christian authors such as Justin Martyr (100-160 CE), never quoted from the four New Testament gospels. In their defence of Christianity against the Gnostics and Jewish and pagan critics, they did not quote from the gospels to support their Christian tenets. There is a good reason—the four gospels were written decades after the life of Jesus.

According to the estimates of modern biblical scholars, such as Dr. Bart Ehrman,[6] professor and department chair of Religious Studies at the University of North Carolina, Chapel Hill, the four gospels were written in Greek (not Aramaic, the language of Jesus) between 70 and 95 CE—40 to 65 years after the life of Jesus! Other theologians, such as John Dominic Crossan[7], date the four gospels later, from the late 70's to early in the second century. What is clear is that we have no eyewitness accounts of Jesus. Instead, we have a gap of two to four generations from the crucifixion of Jesus to the writing of the four New Testament gospels by unknown authors.

---

[6] Ehrman, Bart D. See *Jesus, Interrupted: Revealing the Hidden Contradictions in the Bible (and Why We Don't Know About Them)*. New York: HarperCollins, 2009, 145.

[7] Crossan, John Dominic (professor of Biblical Studies at DePaul University, Chicago) and author of *The Historical Jesus: The Life of a Mediterranean Jewish Peasant*. New York: HarperCollins, 1991, 430, 431.

CHAPTER 2

Are the Four Gospels Historical Documents?

Before I began my humanities programme at the University of Toronto, I had never heard anyone question the authenticity of the New Testament. You have to keep in mind that in 1953, I was only eighteen. There was no internet, and many agnostics and atheists were "closeted." In the subsequent decades, I had the blinders removed from my eyes. I learned that many brilliant people rejected the gospels as historical documents—Edward Gibbon, Baruch Spinoza, Denis Diderot, Abraham Lincoln, Thomas Jefferson, John Dewey, Mark Twain, Bertrand Russell, Thomas Edison, Madelyn Murray O'Hare, Carl Sagan, Katherine Hepburn, Richard Dawkins, Sam Harris, and Christopher Hitchens.

I discovered that even theologians[8] (including my professors at Emmanuel College) did not accept the four gospels as historical biographies. In my first year of theology, I read Albert Schweitzer's *The Quest of the Historical Jesus.* Schweitzer was a medical doctor, musician, theologian, and humanitarian extraordinaire. In this book he compared and analyzed what the four gospels said about Jesus. His goal was to determine whether the gospels were documents of history or faith. In chapter five I will comment in detail on Schweitzer's quest.

We now know much more about how the early Christians viewed Jesus Christ, thanks in part to recent discoveries of "lost" manuscripts.

---

[8] Such as: Allvar Ellegard, Craig Evans, Charles Talbot, E.P. Sanders, Robert M. Grant, Paul Tillich, and Bart Ehrman.

As did Albert Schweitzer, I will compare what the gospels say about *The Jesus Story: His Nativity, Adolescence, Ministry, and Resurrection.* Once you have read this chapter, you will be better able to decide whether or not the Jesus story is one of faith or history. The truth is in the details, and you don't need a degree in theology to examine the details. In addition to comparing the four New Testament gospels, at the end of chapter five, I will summarize two long-lost gospels that most people have never read—the *Gospel of Judas Iscariot,* and the *Gospel of Thomas.*

If you are still undecided about whether or not the New Testament comes under the genre of history or faith, I invite you to examine the earliest manuscripts, as summarized in chapter eight, "Early Christian Texts." It may surprise you to learn that we have no original first century texts of the New Testament gospels, and that the earliest complete manuscripts are from the third and fourth centuries. You may be shocked at the incredible number of differences and discrepancies found in the earliest Greek and Latin manuscripts.

CHAPTER 3

The Jesus Story: His Nativity

When was Jesus Born?

According to Matthew (2:1) Jesus was born when Herod was the king, but according to Luke (2:2), Jesus was born while Quirinius was the governor of Syria. We know, however, from Roman records that Herod died in the year 4 BCE and that Quirinius became the governor of Syria in 6 CE. That is an irreconcilable error of ten years! In 354 CE, Bishop Liberus of Rome chose December 25 as the date for a special Mass to celebrate the birth of Jesus (Christ Mass). It is likely that he chose this date to take the place of the pagan celebrations of the winter solstice, when the northern hemisphere is farthest away from the sun. Actually, no one knows when Jesus was born.

Was Jesus a Descendant of David and Abraham?

Matthew and Luke went to great lengths to prove that Jesus was related to King David and, therefore, had fulfilled messianic prophesies.[9] Each of these gospels lists the genealogy of Jesus by tracing back his lineage through Joseph, the husband of Mary. This is interesting since both

---

[9]   Such as those from Psalm 132:11and Jeremiah 23:5; 33:14-15.

gospels claim that Jesus was born of a virgin; nonetheless, they trace his ancestry back through Joseph!

Have you ever compared these ancestral records found in Matthew 1:1-16 and Luke 3:23-38? I should have done so when I was studying for the ministry. I am embarrassed to admit that I had not noticed the inexplicable differences in these two genealogies until 2009, when I finally compared these two accounts. I discovered that Matthew listed 41 generations from Abraham to Jesus, while Luke listed 57 generations for the same time span!

The author of Luke lists an additional 20 generations, taking us from Abraham back to Adam (the first human according to Genesis, chapter one). Thus in a span of only 77 generations, the author of Luke takes us from Jesus back to Adam! Keeping in mind that our particular species has been in existence for well over 100,000 years, we do not have to be mathematicians to recognize the absurdity of 77 generations! For scientific evidence on the age of Homo sapiens, I recommend the following websites: the National Geographical Magazine, Wikipedia, and the BBC (look for the documentary, *The Incredible Human Journey, Out of Africa*).

Who Visited Jesus in the Manger and How Did They Find Him?

In Matthew's account (2:1-12) wise men (magi) from the East followed a star *till it came to rest over the place where the child was.* The nearest star to us, other than the sun, is Alpha Centauri. With light travelling at 186,300 miles per second, it takes 4.27 light-years for us to see the photons of light from this distant star. If seen on a clear night, it appears as a tiny pinpoint of light, not as a guiding beam. Who were these wise men? Where in the East did they come from? What were their names? There are no collaborating details!

In Luke (2:8-16) an angel tells astounded shepherds that they will find a babe lying in a manger wrapped in swaddling clothes *in the city of David, a Saviour, who is Christ the Lord.* There is no mention of a guiding star. Nor does Luke give us any details of the shepherds. What were their names? How far did they have to travel? How did they locate the manger? Christian tradition harmonizes these two stories into one so that we have this memorable scene of a stable with hay and animals, with Mary, Jesus, and Joseph surrounded by three wise men **and** the shepherds.

The Census (enrolment) of Caesar Augustus

> *In those days a decree went out from Caesar Augustus that all the world should be enrolled. This was the first enrolment, when Quirinius was governor of Syria. And all went to be enrolled, each to his own city. Joseph also went up from Galilee, from the city of Nazareth, to Judea, to the city of David, which is called Bethlehem.* (Luke 2:1-4)

Luke's gospel associates the birth of Jesus to a "worldwide" enrolment that required individuals to return to their birthplaces. Roman authors[10], however, never mentioned a Roman stipulation that in a census taking, everyone in the Roman Empire had to return to their ancestral home! Nor would it make sense. Why would all the male descendants of King David, almost a thousand years after his death, be required by Roman law to go to Bethlehem (the city of David) to be enrolled? In a Roman census, men, as the heads of the household, were responsible for giving census data, not the women. Why then would Mary, a betrothed pregnant woman, have to accompany Joseph for a census taking? It doesn't make sense.

According to Josephus (Jewish historian, soldier and scholar), a census occurred when Quirinius was the Governor of Syria. He described it as a very unpopular, local census, held for taxation purposes in 6 CE. If Josephus was correct, we have a problem because Herod died in the year 4 BCE.

Was Jesus Born in Nazareth or Bethlehem?

The Gospel According to Luke believed that with the birth of Jesus, biblical prophecies about the Messiah were fulfilled. One of these

---

[10]   Such as Josephus (37-100 CE), Titus Livius (Livy) (59 BCE-17 CE), V. Paterculus (19 BCE-31 CE), and Pliny the Elder (23-79 CE).

prophecies said that the long-awaited Messiah would be a Nazarene. *And he (Joseph) went and dwelt in a city called Nazareth, that what was spoken by the prophets might be fulfilled, 'He shall be called a Nazarene'* (Matthew 2:23 and John 1: 45-46). The author of Luke had a dilemma. He knew that Micah had prophesied that the Messiah would come from Bethlehem. *But you, O Bethlehem Ephrathah, who are little to be among the clans of Judah, from you shall come forth for me one who is to be ruler in Israel (Micah 5:2).* But how could Jesus be a Nazarene, if he was born in Bethlehem?

The author of Luke found his answer in the census of the governor Quirinius. Luke used this census to validate both prophecies. Yes, Jesus was born in Bethlehem, but his real home was Nazareth. Thus we have the story of Joseph and Mary travelling from Nazareth, in Galilee, to Bethlehem, the city of King David—a distance of about 80 kilometres. Mary, nine months pregnant, rides on a donkey on a journey that would have taken about four days! The whole journey is incredible and so is the census, because we know that the census of Quirinius occurred ten years after the death of King Herod.

Did King Herod Order the Slaughter of Baby Infants?

Only Matthew recorded this terrible story of Herod who ordered the murder of all the male children in Bethlehem, and the surrounding area. Warned by an angel, Joseph fled to Egypt. It would have been an arduous journey of about 300 kilometres for Mary and her infant son. According to Matthew they remained in Egypt until the death of King Herod. No Roman historian recorded this horrible slaughter—not even Flavius Josephus, who had no reluctance about detailing other atrocities and crimes committed by King Herod.

In the Gospel According to Luke we do not find a single word about the slaughter of the male infants and the flight to Egypt. According to Luke, Mary and Joseph travelled not to Egypt, but to Jerusalem. *And at the end of eight days, when he was circumcised, he was called Jesus . . . and when the time came for their purification according to the Law of Moses, they brought him up to Jerusalem . . .* It is simply impossible to reconcile Matthew's story with that of Luke's account.

One of Matthew's key objectives was to convince Jews that Jesus was the promised Messiah, a fulfillment of the following verse from the prophet Hosea. *When Israel was a child, I loved him and out of Egypt I called my son.* (11:1) As for the slaughter of the male infants, the author of Matthew might have had these words in mind from Jeremiah (31:15). *Thus says the Lord: A voice is heard in Ramah, lamentation and bitter weeping. Rachel is weeping for her children; she refuses to be comforted for her children, because they are not.*

Thus we have Matthew's stories of Herod ordering the slaughter of infants, and Joseph and Mary escaping to Egypt. The author of Matthew was willing to use incredible stories, as long as they helped his readers to accept Jesus as the Christ, the promised Messiah—a sad example of the means justifying the end.

Conclusions

To summarize, conservative Christians believe the nativity stories to be literal, historical truths. It's highly improbable that they will be swayed to think otherwise by the questions I have posed, or the discrepancies I have pointed out. I will likely be dismissed as being anti-Christ, someone in league with the devil, a heretic with a fiery future. Liberal Christians, while perhaps surprised by some of the points I have made, are unlikely to be upset because they do not interpret the nativity stories literally. They understand the Christmas stories with their vivid imagery of a guiding star, angelic hosts, shepherds and wise men bearing gifts, as a beautiful allegory. They see and appreciate the nativity stories through the lens of poetry. Their spiritual focus is to celebrate the birth of Jesus as God's precious gift of love to the world.

No matter how we interpret the nativity stories, there are common grounds for Christians, agnostics and atheists; namely, Christmas is a celebration of family. It is also a time to give, a time to love, and a time to remember the poor, the homeless, and the hungry. More money and food is given to food banks at Christmas than at any other time of the year. As well, there is something universal about the birth of a baby. It is a heartfelt reminder of the joy and hope we feel when a child is born. It is an event that brings out the best in us. Fred Jay expressed this sentiment poignantly when he wrote these lyrics for the hymn, *When a Child Is Born.*

> *A ray of hope flickers in the sky,*
> *A tiny star lights up way on high,*
> *All across the land dawns a brand new morn—*
> *This comes to pass when a child is born.*

CHAPTER 4

The Jesus Story: His Adolescence

There is a veil of mystery over the life of Jesus. Other than one story, which I will outline in this chapter, there are no New Testament details or anecdotes of his life from his birth until he is baptized as an adult by John the Baptist. This is a span of about thirty years.

We are curious about these missing years. Where did Jesus live and what did he do in these three decades? Christians in the early centuries were also interested in this time span of Jesus' life. Bishop Iranaeus[11], in his book *Adversus Haereses*, referred to the childhood of Jesus as told in another gospel of the early centuries—*The Infancy Gospel of Thomas.* The reputed author, the Apostle Thomas, recounted anecdotal, supernatural stories of Jesus—stories that are reminiscent of a Stephen King novel. In one story the boy Jesus made clay birds on the Sabbath and then brought them to life. In another incident a child accidentally bumped into Jesus. Jesus cursed the child and then, depending on which translation you use, threw a stone at him or punched him. The child died! It is an incredulous story showing Jesus misusing his supernatural powers. I mention this pseudo story to show that early Christians loved to speculate about the boy Jesus.

Now, let us examine the one story we do have of the preadolescent Jesus in the Gospel According to Luke, Chapter 2:41-51. In this account,

---

[11]   Iranaeus (120 to 200 CE) is the third early Christian author described in Addendum A.

Jesus travelled with his parents to Jerusalem to celebrate the Passover, a religious festival commemorating the Jewish Exodus from Egypt. This event was celebrated in Jerusalem for seven days. In Jesus' time, the population of Jerusalem was c. 25,000, but at Passover this number would quadruple.

> *Now his parents went to Jerusalem every year at the feast of the Passover. And when he was twelve years old, they went up according to custom; and when the feast was ended, as they were returning, the boy Jesus stayed behind in Jerusalem. His parents did not know it, but supposing him to be in the company they went a day's journey, and they sought him among their kinsfolk and acquaintances; and when they did not find him, they returned to Jerusalem, seeking him. After three days they found him in the temple, sitting among the teachers, listening to them and asking them questions; and all who heard him were amazed at his understanding and his answers. And when they saw him they were astonished; and his mother said to him, 'Son, why have you treated us so? Behold your father and I have been looking for you anxiously.' And he said to them, 'How is it that you sought me? Did you not know that I must be in my Father's house?' And they did not understand the saying which he spoke to them. And he went down with them and came to Nazareth, and was obedient to them; and his mother kept all these things in her heart."*

This interesting story raises a host of questions. How did Mary and Joseph travel to Jerusalem and with whom? In this crowded city where did they stay? Why did they allow their 12-year-old son to be unsupervised in a city of 100,000? Why did they begin their journey home without him? Why did it take a whole day on their way home to miss him? When they returned to Jerusalem, they found him in the temple surrounded by rabbis. What did Jesus say that amazed these religious leaders? Why did Mary chastise Jesus? Had she forgotten her miraculous conception, and the angelic message that her son was destined to be a great spiritual leader? Why was Jesus so curt and abrupt to his mother? He had not seen Mary or Joseph for four days. Did it not occur to him that they would be fraught with worry?

Perhaps I am being unfair to expect journalistic details from someone writing in the first century of the Christian era. On the other hand, this lack of details is a strong clue that the story was written years after the event—and not by an eyewitness. The most likely explanation for the scarcity of details is that the story was passed on by oral tradition long before it was written. If that is the case, details tend to be forgotten, omitted or exaggerated in the telling and the retelling. Facts become blurred.

Did a boy, 12 years of age, astound learned rabbis by his questions and answers? Perhaps. There may well be some basis to this story, but to hold the story (recorded only in Luke's gospel) to be historically inerrant is indeed a leap of faith.

CHAPTER 5

The Jesus Story: His Ministry

Albert Schweitzer in his book, *The Quest of the Historical Jesus,* observed that every person has his or her own view of who Jesus was. Let us see if this is true, starting with the authors of the four gospels of the New Testament, as well as the authors of two gospels that never made it into the New Testament—the Gospel of Thomas and the Gospel of Judas Iscariot. Are all these perspectives of Jesus similar or are there distinct differences?

The Ministry of Jesus According to Mark

The name Mark occurs in Acts 12 and in 2 Timothy 4:11. This Mark was a contemporary of Peter and Paul. Irenaeus (120-200 CE), the Bishop of Lyons, France, made the following reference to a Mark in *Against Heresies 3.1.1. After their death* (referring to Peter and Paul) *Mark, the disciple and interpreter of Peter, transmitted to us in writing what was preached by Peter.* Both Peter and Paul were martyred c. 67 CE during the rule of the Roman Emperor Nero. The life span of Jesus (based on the historical records we have of King Herod and Pontius Pilate) would have been from c.5 BCE to c.30 CE. Consequently, if the author of this gospel is the Mark of Acts and Timothy, he would have written his story of Jesus about 40 years **after** the ministry of Jesus.

Mark's story of Jesus begins, not with the virgin birth and nativity stories, but with Jesus as an adult being baptized in the River Jordan by John the Baptist. It is a brief account with few supporting details. He makes no reference to the precise location of the baptism, the time of day, or the names of any who witnessed this important event. He tells his story in the third person, as do the other gospel writers. None of Mark's stories begin with "I" or "we".

After his baptism Jesus passes along the Sea of Galilee, and as he does he calls four fishermen to follow him—Simon, Andrew, James and John (1:17). Mark gives us no specifics about the village(s) they came from, their marital status, or age. Geographical and personal information are missing. We wonder if Jesus said more to them than what we find in Mark 1:17. *Follow me and I will make you become fishers of men.* Was one statement all it took for them to drop everything to follow someone they hadn't met before?

Mark's gospel does not follow a chronological order. It is a collection of stories with only a few parables. It has neither a Sermon on the Mount nor the Lord's Prayer. Details are missing, not only because this gospel was written years after the life of Jesus, but also because the author is focused on the message; namely, that Jesus is the long-awaited Messiah and the Kingdom of God is at hand.

In this gospel Jesus speaks and acts with authority. He heals the sick and battles evil spirits (Mark 1:32-39). Twice, he miraculously feeds a multitude with a few fish and a few loaves of bread (6:35-44 and 8:1-9). He casts out demons; he heals lepers; he calls for repentance; he forgives sinners; he warns of the imminent judgment of God (2:17).

Mark's Jesus is neither mild nor meek. In chapter 1:40-43, Jesus heals a leper and then "sternly charged him" (other translations say "severely rebuked him") not to tell anyone of what just happened. We see another instance of his anger in chapter 3:5. As Jesus is about to heal a man with a crippled hand, he is confronted by Pharisees who are upset because he is about to heal someone on the Sabbath. This is a violation of Jewish law! Jesus reacts with anger. "And he looked around at them with anger, grieved at their hardness of heart." A third instance occurs in Mark 10:14. Jesus is clearly annoyed with his disciples for scolding parents who were bringing their children for him to bless. It is interesting to note that when Matthew and Luke recount these same stories, they either tone down the references to anger or omit it altogether.

Mark's Jesus believed in an imminent apocalypse. A*s he came out of the temple, one of his disciples said to him, 'Look, Teacher, what wonderful stones and what wonderful buildings!' And Jesus said to him, 'Do you see these great buildings? There shall not be left here one stone upon another that will not be thrown down.' (*Mark 13:1-2).

Keeping in mind that this gospel was written about 40 years **after** the ministry of Jesus, and that the Romans razed the Temple to the ground in 70 CE, it is likely the Jerusalem Temple already lay in ruins when the author of Mark wrote these two verses.

In Mark's Gospel Jesus, in his final hours before his arrest, prays in the Garden of Gethsemane. Jesus is greatly distressed and troubled. He falls to his knees and prays to God three times "to remove this cup from me". After his arrest and trial, he is silent as he is taken to Golgotha to be crucified. He says nothing to the two robbers who are also crucified, one on each side of him. Just before he dies he calls out in a loud voice these shocking words that epitomize his loneliness and sense of abandonment: *My God, my God, why hast thou forsaken me?* (15:34). As we shall see, Luke and John have very different accounts of Jesus in his last hours.

The Ministry of Jesus According to Matthew

When the author of Matthew wrote his story of Jesus, he had two main sources, the Gospel According to Mark, and an earlier document containing teachings of Jesus. Some scholars speculate that this latter document is likely "The Sayings of Jesus", a copy of which was found in 1945 in Egypt, at Nag Hammadi. In the "Sayings of Jesus" we find parables, the Lord's Prayer and the Beatitudes. It does not mention his crucifixion or resurrection.

Matthew's author sometimes copied Mark word for word. At other times, he changed what Mark wrote. Following are two examples of textual changes. In Mark 3:1-5, Jesus is about to heal a man with a withered hand on the Sabbath under the critical eye of Pharisees. Jesus defends himself with one question. *Is it lawful on the Sabbath to do good or to do harm, to save life or to kill? But they were silent. And he looked around at them with anger . . ."* Matthew's account (12:9-14) is longer and different. Here Jesus answers the Pharisees as follows: *What man of you, if he has one sheep, and it falls into a pit on the Sabbath, will not lay hold of it and lift it out? Of how much more value is a man than a sheep! So it is lawful to do good on the Sabbath.* Matthew had no qualms about expanding on what Mark had written, or leaving out negative details such as Jesus being angry.

Matthew has an impelling message for Jews. He makes 15 references to Jesus fulfilling the prophecies of the Old Testament. The references begin with words such as: *This was to fulfill what was spoken by the prophet . . .* The author of Matthew knew his Old Testament and, more so than the other gospels, makes frequent references to the prophets to convince his Jewish audience that Jesus is the Christ—the anointed one, the Messiah.

Matthew's Gospel makes it quite clear (5:17-19) that while salvation comes through the death and resurrection of Jesus, Jewish law is still very important. *For truly I say to you, till heaven and earth pass away, not an iota, not a dot, will pass away from the law until all is accomplished.* He is the harshest of the gospel writers in blaming Jews for the crucifixion. Only Matthew relates the story at Jesus' trial of the Jewish crowd crying out, *His blood be upon us and our children* (Matthew27:25). Sadly and shamefully, this statement was destined to be used for centuries by bigots to rationalize their ill-treatment of Jews.

The Ministry of Jesus According to Luke

The author of Luke used both Mark and very likely *The Sayings of Jesus* as his source material. In many places, Luke's story of Jesus is identical with that of Mark, word for word. In other instances, he modifies what Mark wrote. For example, when Luke tells the story of Jesus healing the man with the crippled hand on the Sabbath (Luke 6:6-11), he says that the Pharisees were watching, as well as "scribes". Thus, he adds a new audience. Like Matthew, he says nothing about the anger of Jesus; instead he ascribes anger to the watching religious critics.

Although Luke's gospel has many similarities to those of Mark and Matthew, the author of Luke has his own particular emphases. He stresses the importance of prayer more so than the other gospels. He mentions an angel or angels 20 times; whereas there are only five references in Mark. Luke mentions the Holy Ghost (Holy Spirit) 12 times as compared to Mark's four references. But the most striking difference is Luke's portrayal of Jesus as one who is almost always in control, composed, and compassionate. There is only one passage where this is not the case. In Luke 22:39-46, Jesus prays at the Mount of Olives just before his arrest: *Father, if thou art willing, remove this cup from me; nevertheless, not my will, but thine, be done.* In many manuscripts the following verses are found (unique to this gospel). *And being in an agony he prayed more earnestly; and his sweat became like great drops of blood falling down upon the ground.* It has long been noted by New Testament scholars that some of the earliest Greek manuscripts of Alexandria make no mention of this "agony" and "bloody sweat". These disputed verses (22:43-44) may well have been added by a later scribe who was trying to harmonize Luke's account with that of Mark.

Note how Jesus goes to his death in Luke's gospel. In Mark, as he is led to the cross and crucified, he says nothing until just before he dies when he calls out, *My God, my God, why hast thou forsaken me?* But in Luke's account, Jesus, on route to his crucifixion, speaks to a group of women who are weeping for him. *Daughters of Jerusalem, do not weep for me, but weep for yourselves, and your children* (23:28-31). After his crucifixion, hanging from the cross, Jesus says, *Father forgive them; for they know not what they do* (23:34). In Mark, Jesus says nothing to the two robbers crucified one on each side of him. In Matthew, both criminals revile Jesus. But in Luke (24:39-43) one of the criminals speaks out defending Jesus, and Jesus says, *Truly I say to you, today you will be with me in Paradise.* But the really striking contrasts with Mark's account are the last words of Jesus in Luke's gospel: *Father, into thy hands I commit my spirit (24:46).* Jesus dies not despairingly, but calmly and confidently.

The Ministry of Jesus According to John

The Gospels According to Matthew, Mark and Luke are often referred to as the Synoptic gospels because of their similarities. The Gospel According to John, however, stands by itself—different in many ways as we shall see. This gospel proclaims Jesus as divine from the very first chapter. He is not only the Messiah; he is also the Son of God.

It is different too in its omissions. There is no mention of the Virgin birth, the nativity stories, hell, the parables, the Lord's Prayer, the Sermon on the Mount, the casting out of demons, or the Last Supper. It has new material. In chapter two Jesus turns water into wine at the wedding in Cana; in chapter three, Jesus speaks at length with Nicodemus (a Pharisee who becomes a secret follower); in chapter four, Jesus carries on a lengthy conversation with a Samaritan woman at the well, and in chapter ten, he raises Lazareth from the dead.

The most remarkable addition, however, is the story of a woman accused of adultery, and about to be stoned to death for her sin (John 8:1-11). We immediately feel sorry for her, and not just because of the severity of her punishment (based on Leviticus 20:10). We wonder why she is the only one about to be punished. What about the man who was caught with her? Even so, it is an inspiring story, portraying Jesus as caring, forgiving and very wise. Jesus saves her with one comment: *Let him who is without sin among you be the first to throw a stone at her.* Regretfully, because it is a good story, this incident was added much later. We know this to be the case because this story is missing from four of our earliest texts—Papyrus 66 dated c. 200, Papyrus 75 of the third century, and two complete manuscripts[12] of the fourth century (Codex Sinaiticus and Codex Vaticanus).

The vocabulary and style of John's gospel is different from the synoptic gospels. In the latter, Jesus speaks with brevity letting the listener discover the meaning of his parables. In John's gospel, Jesus repetitively expounds on his themes. For example, in chapter six Jesus feeds 5,000 men (no women and children in this account) with five loaves and two fish. The next day Jesus explains this event, and its spiritual significance in great detail to his disciples. He concludes his explanation with these words: *I am the bread of life; he who comes to me shall not hunger and he who believes in me shall never thirst* (6:35).

You may recall the story of Jesus cleansing the temple. He makes a whip of cords and drives out the money changers and those selling pigeons, sheep, and oxen. This incident occurs at the very beginning of his ministry in John, but in Matthew, Mark, and Luke it happens at the end of his ministry, just hours before his arrest. Some Christians try to explain away this difference by saying that Jesus cleansed the temple twice. It is an unlikely explanation because in John's account there is no arrest or angry protest from the chief priests and scribes.

---

[12] See chapter eight, *Early Texts.*

John's gospel has a different account of Jesus' last hours. According to Mark, chapters 14 and 15, Jesus is crucified the day **after** the Passover, but in John's gospel Jesus is crucified on the day **before** the Passover. (John 19:14). In both Mark and John, Pontius Pilate asks Jesus if he is the King of the Jews. In Mark, Jesus replies, *You have said so (Mark 15:2)*, but in John's gospel, Jesus answers Pilate very differently. He says, *My kingship is not of this world; if my kingship were of this world my servants would fight, that I might not be handed over to the Jews . . . For this I was born, and for this I have come into the world, to bear witness to the truth* (18:33-37).

In Mark, Jesus dies alone with Mary Magdalene, Mary the mother of James, and Salome looking on from afar, but in John's gospel the women (and one male disciple) are close enough that he can address them. In Mark's gospel, Jesus' last words are, *My God, my God, why hast thou forsaken me?* In John, Jesus dies saying, *It is finished.* He dies composed and in control.

Conclusions

I began this chapter with Albert Schweitzer's comment that every person has his or her own perspective of Jesus. Is this true of the gospels of Matthew, Mark, Luke, and John? I think so. They are significantly different in content and theology.

It must also be said that the gospel authors had no qualms about quoting from each other and from others without acknowledging their sources. Consequently, these gospels have much in common: Jesus teaches with divine authority; Jesus forgives sin; Jesus believes in demons and angels; Jesus is crucified; Jesus is resurrected—except for the Gospel According to Mark. The oldest and most reliable manuscripts[13] of Mark end with the mystery of an empty tomb. In each gospel, Jesus believes that the end is near[14]—an apocalyptic end! The gospels present Jesus as the long-awaited Messiah, the fulfillment of the prophetic promises. The Jesus of Matthew, Mark, Luke and John is much more than a teacher.

---

[13]   *Sinaiticus and Vaticanus.* See Chapter 8—*Early Christian Texts.*

[14]   See Mark 9:1, Matthew 16:28, John 5:28.

The Ministry of Jesus According to the Gospel of Judas Iscariot

It may be news to you that we now have a gospel manuscript supposedly written by Judas Iscariot! It was discovered near the city of El Minya, close to the Nile River in the late 1970s. Scholars knew it once existed, because Iranaeus, Bishop of Lyons, denounced this gospel in his book, *Against Heresies* which he wrote c.180 CE. So it was with great excitement that biblical scholars awaited its translation.

Three experts from the National Geographical Society carefully examined the brittle 26 pages of this papyrus manuscript. Timothy Jull, a specialist in carbon 14 dating, determined that the document had been written c. 280 CE (plus or minus sixty years). Professor Stephen Emmel, an expert linguist, translated this Coptic document into English. He determined the Coptic manuscript to be a translation of an earlier Greek document. Bart Ehrman, a New Testament scholar renowned for his knowledge of early Christian texts, assessed its historical and theological significance.[15]

In the four New Testament gospels, Judas is shown as a villain and traitor who betrayed Jesus to the Romans for 30 pieces of silver. According to Matthew 27:5, Judas hung himself immediately after he betrayed Jesus for thirty pieces of silver. In Acts 1:18 there is a different version of his demise. After buying a field with his ill-begotten money, Judas goes into the field, *and falling headlong he burst open in the middle and his bowels gushed out.* These are obviously two conflicting accounts.

In this lost gospel, however, Judas is depicted as a close and trusted friend of Jesus, an obedient confidant. He is the only disciple who realizes that Jesus wants to die, not to atone for the sins of humanity, but to be free of his earthly body, free to return to the spiritual realm. This perspective in the Gospel of Judas Iscariot is one of the main tenets of Christian Gnosticism, which will be examined more fully in chapter 7, *Early Christian Authors (100 to 400).*

This once lost gospel is important for a number of reasons. Firstly, it is additional proof that by the second and third centuries, there was a great diversity of opinions about Jesus, and the events surrounding his ministry. We know that in the early centuries of Christianity, there were

---

[15]   See Ehrman, Bart D. *The Lost Gospel of Judas Iscariot.* Oxford: Oxford University Press, Inc., 2006.

as many as twenty gospels! Secondly, it is obvious that church leaders like Iranaeus, not only disavowed the Gospel of Judas Iscariot as heretical, but tried to suppress its reading, as well as other "Christian" writings with which they disagreed. Fortunately, many "lost" texts have been found. The most important discovery occurred in 1945, near the Egyptian village of Nag Hammadi. Here, an Arab farmer unearthed a red earthenware jar containing 52 Gnostic texts including a **complete** text of the Gospel of Thomas! We can therefore say with certainty, that Christian Gnosticism was popular and widespread in early Christian communities.

The Ministry of Jesus According to the Gospel of Thomas

This Gospel contains 114 sayings of Jesus. There is no mention of his birth and baptism, his miracles, his crucifixion, or his resurrection. One half of the sayings are similar to those of the New Testament gospels, but they are briefer and more succinct. This is a gospel that focuses solely on the teachings of Jesus. Here, as with the Gospel of Judas Iscariot, there is a Gnostic perspective—salvation comes not through the death and resurrection of Jesus, but by special secret knowledge that comes through a correct interpretation of the sayings of Jesus. For example the first "saying" is as follows:

> *These are the secret sayings which the living Jesus spoke and which Didymus Judas Thomas wrote down. And he said, "Whoever finds the interpretation of these sayings will not experience death."*

There are people today who say they are Christians, not because they believe in the Apostles' Creed, but because they believe in the teachings of Jesus. In this gospel they have a precedent—Gnostic Christians who believed that the key to a saving relationship with God, as well as eternal life, was "the sayings of Jesus". For a scholarly analysis of the Gospel of Thomas I recommend Bart Ehrman's *Lost Christianities: The Battle for Scripture and the Faiths We Never Knew.* Oxford: Oxford University Press, 2003, pages 55 to 65.

CHAPTER 6

The Jesus Story: His Resurrection

Prior to my ordination, I was interviewed by the Committee of Colleges and Students. Their mandate was to determine whether I should be ordained. It was intimidating. What questions would they ask me? What if they didn't like my answers? The interview day arrived, and I found myself, along with several of my classmates, sitting outside a conference room nervously waiting my turn. One of my classmates asked me if I was worried about any particular issue. I said I hoped no one would ask me about the Virgin Birth. When I asked him if he had any concerns, he too had one—the Trinity. Much to his amusement, I replied that I hadn't thought too much about that one.

As I look back at our conversation I find it interesting that neither of us mentioned the resurrection of Christ. Perhaps it never occurred to us that we would be questioned on such a central, sacrosanct doctrine as that of the resurrection. I am embarrassed to admit it, but it had never occurred to me to compare the different accounts of the resurrection in the four gospels, and in the Apostle Paul's letter to the Corinthians. It is surprising, to say the least, what you find when you compare these five texts.

Who went to the tomb on the Sunday following the Crucifixion?

Mark's gospel (16:1) mentions three women, Mary Magdalene, Mary the mother of James, and Salome. According to Matthew there were two women, Mary Magdalene, and the other Mary. Luke has an indefinite number of women—Mary Magdalene, Joanna, Mary the mother of James, and "the other women" (24:10). John says that Mary Magdalene came first, alone. It is strange that there is no consistency in these gospel reports, and that none of them mentions Mary, the mother of Jesus. In 1 Corinthians 15:5, the Apostle Paul makes no mention of **any** women coming to the empty tomb. He states simply that Jesus appeared to Cephas (another name for Peter), and then to the 12 apostles. Why does Paul not mention the women? Were they not important witnesses?

Whom did they see at the tomb on that first Sunday?

Mark writes that they saw a young man dressed in a white robe (16.5). Matthew says it was an angel, radiant and white (28.2). Luke tells us that there were two men *"in dazzling apparel"* (24.4). John records that there were two angels dressed in white. These are small differences, but the point is that we do not know whether they saw one or two individuals. Nor do we know whether they saw a man or an angel.

What message was given to the women at the empty tomb?

In Matthew and Mark, the women are told not to be afraid, that Jesus is risen from the dead, that they are to tell this to his disciples, and that Jesus will go before them into Galilee where they will see him. In Luke there is only one message—that Jesus has risen. In John's gospel (20.13) there is only a question, *"Woman, why are you weeping?"*

Who saw Jesus and where?

In Mark 16:8 Mary Magdalene, Mary the mother of James, and Salome flee from the empty tomb trembling and astonished by the dramatic news told to them by the young man dressed in white. There is no mention of a risen Christ—only the drama of an empty tomb. In other ancient, but less reliable texts, there are eleven additional verses added after Mark 16:8.[16] In these "additional" verses, Jesus appears first to Mary Magdalene. Then *he appeared in another form to two of them, as they were walking in the country . . . afterwards he appeared to the eleven themselves as they sat at table* (16:12, 14). There is no mention in these latter verses of the disciples going to Galilee.

In Matthew's gospel, as Mary Magdalene and the other Mary run to find the disciples to tell them what has happened, they meet and recognize Jesus. When the disciples hear of this encounter with Jesus, the disciples go to Galilee, to the mountain to which Jesus had directed them, and there they too see Jesus. (28:8-10)

In Luke, Jesus appears first to two unnamed followers who are on their way to the village Emmaus, about seven miles from Jerusalem. It is a strange encounter. Although they speak at length with Jesus and invite him to stay overnight, it is not until they sit down to eat and he blesses the bread, that they recognize him. They immediately return to Jerusalem to tell the eleven disciples that Jesus has risen and has been seen by Peter. *And as they were saying this, Jesus himself stood among them"* (24:36). Here Jesus appears to the disciples in Jerusalem—contradicting the angelic message in Matthew and Mark that the disciples were to go to Galilee to see Jesus.

In John's gospel, Jesus first appears to Mary Magdalene. Although he carries on a conversation with her, she fails to recognize him until he says her name. The same evening ten disciples are in a locked room (presumably still in Jerusalem). Suddenly, Jesus appears in their midst (John 20.11-19). Eight days later at the same house, with the doors shut as before, Jesus suddenly appears again. He has come so that the previously absent Thomas can see and feel his pierced hands and side, and believe (21:28).

---

[16] In chapter 8 I will examine this later and longer ending.

Conclusions

As a theological student, I suspect I had unconsciously ignored the many differences and inconsistencies in these "eyewitness" accounts of the resurrection. Who knows with any certainty who accompanied Mary Magdalene to the tomb? Was there one angel at the tomb or two? What did they say to the women? Did the disciples first see the risen Christ in Galilee or Jerusalem?

We have already noted Paul's account, in 1 Corinthians 15:5, that Jesus appeared to Peter and his disciples. In the following verses, Paul wrote that Jesus appeared to more than 500 brethren at one time! Where did this remarkable "appearance" occur? Exactly when did it happen? What was the reaction of the 500 witnesses? If such a spectacular event happened, why did no Jewish or Roman writer ever mention it?

Mark, Matthew and Luke use almost identical language to say that on the day when Jesus was crucified, there was darkness over the whole land from the sixth to the ninth hour.[17] The author of John mentions the sixth hour as the time when Pilate handed over Jesus to the chief priests to be crucified, but he makes no reference to any darkness that covered the whole land (John 19:14). A strange omission! In Matthew's account the darkness was followed by **other** miraculous events.

> *the earth shook, and the rocks were split; the tombs also were opened, and many bodies of the saints who had fallen asleep were raised, and coming out of the tombs after his resurrection they went into the holy city and appeared to many.* (27:51-53).

Again, it is strange that Mark, Luke, John and the Apostle Paul omit these amazing events. Nor is there one word from the Jewish or Roman writers of this era. Philo (20 BCE to 50 CE) was a renown Jewish writer/philosopher who wrote about this period of Jewish history, and his home was close to Jerusalem. The Roman historians Tacitus (56-120 CE) and Plutarch (45-125) were prolific authors; yet neither of them had anything to say about the darkness that covered the whole land from the sixth to the ninth hour. Nor did they report the extraordinary news of

---

[17]   See Mark 15:33, Luke 23:44, and Matthew 27:45.

an earthquake, and dead people coming to life, leaving their tombs, and being seen by many in Jerusalem.

One important point that usually goes unnoticed is that the events of the Passion Story are all crowded into a time span of 24 hours. The Passion Story is the term used for all the incidents listed in the gospels from the Last Supper to the crucifixion. According to the gospels, this is what happened.

After the Last Supper, Jesus retired to the Garden of Gethsemane to pray. The disciples, instead of watching over Jesus, fell asleep three times. Then Judas betrayed him and Jesus is hauled away for his trials. The first trial was convened by the High Priest Caiaphas, with the chief priests, scribes and elders attending. As soon as it was morning, the chief priests and elders decided that Jesus should be executed. They tied Jesus up and took him to Pontius Pilate, the Roman Governor of Judea. According to Luke, when Pilate learned that Jesus was a Galilean, he sent Jesus to Herod (Antipas), the Jewish ruler of Galilee. Herod tried to question a silent Jesus, listened to the accusations of the chief priests, and then sent Jesus "in gorgeous apparel" back to Pilate. That was a clever tactic of Herod—his way of saying that only Pilate could deal with someone claiming to be a king. Pilate reluctantly submitted to the will of the accusers and ordered the execution. Jesus, after being whipped, began his long walk to Golgotha, staggering under the weight of the cross, to be crucified. Jesus died at about the ninth hour.

Although it's not impossible, it's hard to imagine that all these events (particularly three trials) could have occurred in one evening and one day. It is also difficult to imagine Pontius Pilate being intimidated by the High Priest and his entourage. The gospels represent Pilate as vacillating and weak. Yet, we know from Roman history, that was not the case. In fact, Pilate was eventually called back to Rome to answer charges that he was too oppressive and severe to the Jews.

With so many glaring inconsistencies, it should come as no surprise that many people have decided that the resurrection is myth, not history. So do scholars such as John Robinson, Bishop of Woolwich who wrote *Honest to God*, Tom Harpur, an Anglican priest and author of *The Pagan Christ*, and Acharya S., archaeologist, historian, mythologist and linguist. Acharya, in chapter 12 of his book *Suns of God* gives an extensive list of religious and secular scholars who have rejected the resurrection as being historically true.

When we examine the details of the resurrection as found in the gospels and in Paul's first letter to the Corinthians, we find a plethora of discrepancies and inconsistencies. When we look at the Passion Story under the microscope of reason, it is very, very difficult to read the story as history. For many this realization must be confusing and discouraging. This can happen, if we take the Passion Story literally.

I have already noted that Paul never mentions Jesus in a historical sense. He gives us no biographical details of Jesus of Nazareth. He makes no reference to his Virgin Birth, his parables, or his miracles. Not once in his epistles to the early Christian communities does he mention something that Jesus did or said. The apostle Paul, however, had much to say about Christ living on in us. In his epistles he focused on a spiritual Christ.

> *Christ in you, the hope of glory* (Colossians 1:27). I have *been crucified with Christ; it is no longer I who live but Christ who lives in me (Colossians 2:20). For the whole law is fulfilled in one word, 'You shall love your neighbor as yourself'* (Colossians 5:13). *The fruit of the Spirit is love, joy, peace, patience, kindness, goodness, faithfulness, gentleness, self-control* (Colossians 5:22).

Clement of Alexandria (c.150-215 CE) believed that scripture should be understood as myth and allegory, and not interpreted literally. So did Origen, another esteemed early Church Father. He was the head of the Catechetical School of Alexandria from 203 to 231 CE. In his *De Principiis,* he wrote a comprehensive Christian philosophy. Origen said it was heresy to interpret the crucifixion and resurrection literally!

Did the gospel writers intend their resurrection stories to be understood as spiritual metaphors? The nativity stories told by Matthew and Luke only make sense when read as allegories. Is this how they intended their resurrection stories to be understood? Were they trying to tell us that even though Jesus had been crucified, dead and laid to rest in a tomb, he was still alive in the mind and hearts of those who loved him? This spiritual interpretation has been made by many Christians, past and present. In one of his concluding paragraphs in "The Quest of the Historical Jesus", Albert Schweitzer wrote, *Jesus as a concrete historical personality remains a mystery to our time, but his Spirit, which lies hidden in His words, is known for its simplicity, and its influence is direct.*

CHAPTER 7

Early Christian Authors (100 to 400)

Priests and pastors seldom write or speak about the Christian authors of the early centuries of Christianity. This silence is unfortunate because in these important, formative years there were heated battles over what to believe and who to believe. In Addendum **A**, I have noted seven authors who helped determine what Christians were to believe—Justin Martyr 100-165, Marcion 100-60, Iranaeus 120-200, Tertullian 160-220, Clement of Alexandria 150-215, Origen 185-254, and Eusebius 260-340. From my summaries of these authors, you will appreciate the doctrinal battles that were waged. You will understand why 250 bishops came together at the Council of Nicaea, in 325 CE, to define what Christians should believe.

One of the most controversial issues was that of **Gnosticism** (from the Greek word *gnosis* meaning knowledge). There were numerous Gnostic sects in the Middle East. Gnostics who became Christians frequently tried to integrate some of their prior beliefs with their new religion, Christianity—much to the chagrin of many early Christian leaders. Following are some of the Gnostic beliefs that were viewed with great consternation.

- The earth was created by a deity who had been expelled from heaven. Consequently, all matter was evil.
- There was more than one God. The God of the Old Testament was a vengeful law maker. In sharp contrast, the God of the New Testament was a God of love and mercy.

- Salvation from this evil world was possible through secret, intuitive knowledge from Jesus. This divine, mystical gnosis, once experienced, was a life-changing catalyst.
- Some Gnostics (believing that all matter was evil) could not conceive of Jesus as fully human. To them it was impossible that Jesus, the divine Son of God, could suffer and bleed. They resolved this dilemma with a doctrine we call Docetism (from the Greek word "dokein" meaning "to seem"). Jesus only appeared to be human; he only seemed to suffer and die.
- Gnostics tended to interpret scripture spiritually and symbolically; e.g., some interpreted the resurrection of Christ spiritually not physically; while the body of Christ had perished, his spirit lived on—a spirit that his followers could incorporate and experience.

The Council of Nicaea (Turkey)

We know from authors such as Eusebius, that more than 250 bishops attended the Council of Nicaea. Eusebius was there in his role as bishop and historian. In all likelihood, Constantine I, the Roman emperor, convened this council hoping Christianity would bring much needed stability and peace to the Roman Empire. The bishops also had a monumental objective—to unify the various churches and cults under one universal, Catholic Church. To do so they needed to resolve some major controversies, formulate a Christian creed, and define church policies.

The most contentious issue of the day concerned the nature of Christ. Arius, a Christian priest in Alexandria, was a popular theologian and able debater. He argued passionately that while Jesus was the Son of God, there was a time when the Son did not exist; he believed Jesus to have been created by God, the Father, and thus was not equal to God. Arius saw Jesus, not as a literal Son, but as a figurative Son. The vast majority of the bishops differed, arguing that Jesus Christ was equal and co-eternal with God the Father. At the conclusion of the debate, all but two of the bishops voted against Arius, who was then declared a heretic. The two bishops who did not condemn Arius were exiled and **anathematized.** I try to avoid theological jargon, but this is a rather interesting word. It is from a Greek word meaning to detest. So in a literal sense, the dissenting bishops were ecclesiastically detested! In practical terms they were excommunicated.

By the end of this council, the bishops, in addition to passing 20 canons (decrees), had formulated the Nicene Creed, a summary of basic Christian tenets. Following is the section of the creed that defined the nature of Christ, worded very carefully to refute the Arian position. *We believe in one Lord, Jesus Christ, the only Son of God, eternally begotten of the Father, God from God, Light from Light, true God from true God, begotten, not made, one in Being with the Father.* Chrystal clear. Right?

Concluding Observations

In the debates of the second century, early authors such as Justin Martyr, Iranaeus, and Tertullian did not quote from the gospels of Matthew, Mark, Luke or John! In their defence of Christianity against the Gnostics, and Jewish and pagan critics, they made no mention of the Virgin Birth, the Lord's Prayer, the raising of Lazareth from the dead, the parables, the turning of water into wine, the miraculous healing of lepers, Jesus walking on water and stilling the angry waves, or his inspiring Sermon on the Mount (which includes the Beatitudes). There are logical explanations for these omissions. The four gospels of the New Testament were written decades after the life of Jesus and it took many years for their dissemination as sacred texts.

The early authors that I have examined gave us no personal details of Jesus' life, his mother Mary, his childhood, his brothers and sisters, his adolescence, or his employment. Nor did they give details about his physical appearance: his physique, his height, his hair, or any distinguishing facial characteristics. This is not surprising because with the passage of time, personal details are usually forgotten or lost.

Not all Gnostic teachings were incompatible with Christianity. The gospel account of the temptations of Jesus[18] is a clear example of a dualism between the heavenly deity Jesus, and the fallen deity, Satan. The Kingdom of God is one of Light and Love, but the world is beset by darkness, sin and tribulation; e.g., *We know we are of God, and the whole*

---

[18]   Matthew 4:1-11.

world is in the power of the evil one (1 John 5:19). *Behold the Lamb of God who takes away the sin of the world* (John 1:29); *in the world you have tribulation . . .* (John 16:33). Paul, in his letters to the early churches, often uses the secret, mystical language of the Gnostics; e.g., *Jesus Christ, the revelation of the mystery which was kept secret for long ages . . .* (Romans 16:25); *We impart a secret and hidden wisdom of God . . .* (1 Corinthians 2:7). Paul's focus is not on the Jesus of Nazareth, nor on Jesus' parables and miracles, but on the spiritual "Christos", a term he uses over two hundred times—Christ within you.

As did the Apostles Peter and Paul, the early Christian authors exhorted the Jewish communities to accept Jesus as their Messiah, and to believe that salvation came, not through obedience to the Jewish Law, but through faith in the risen Christ. When this message "fell on deaf ears," they castigated Jews as murderers of God. Unfortunately, in doing so they sowed the seeds for centuries of blame, resentment, and persecution.

The Council of Nicaea set a grim precedent for dealing with heretics—one that lasted for hundreds of years. Arius was condemned as a heretic, excommunicated and exiled. The emperor decreed that all his writings were to be burned. By the end of the fourth century, even the once revered names of Clement and Origen were added to the list of heretics, and their writings, banned and burned. Those found reading the manuscripts of these two founding fathers risked excommunication!

The Nicene Creed, with minor modifications, is known today as the Apostles' Creed. The title implies that these statements of faith came from the first apostles, thus adding more weight and credibility to the creed. We know that is not the case. The wording was that of the bishops of the fourth century. The two priests sent to represent the bishop of Rome played a minor role at the Council of Nicaea. As I reviewed the records of this council, I saw no acknowledgement that the bishop of Rome was regarded as the successor of Peter, and, consequently, the head of the Catholic Church.

In the second and third century, the Christian Church was at an important theological crossroad. Should Christians interpret scripture using the symbolic, allegorical approach of Clement and Origen, or, like Eusebius, should they interpret scripture as literal, historical truth? The latter perspective became the norm. It was much easier for the largely, uneducated congregations to understand a literal gospel, presented as history. Several prominent Fathers of the Church said as much. St. Gregory of Nazianzen (329 to 389 CE) in a letter to St. Jerome wrote as follows.

> *Nothing can impose better on the people than verbiage; the less they understand, the more they admire. Our Fathers and Doctors have often said, not what they thought, but what circumstance and necessity forced them to.* St. Augustine (354 to 430 CE) in his book *City of God* expressed a similar sentiment. *There are certain things that are true which it is not useful for the vulgar crowd to know; and certain things which although they are false it is expedient for the people to believe otherwise.*

Thus, as early as the fourth century the die was cast. Christians were to accept the Old Testament stories as literal, historical truths. The world was created in six days; Noah built an ark big enough for pairs of all earth's creatures; the Great Flood covered the whole earth because God had decided to eliminate a sinful generation; Jonah lived in the belly of a great fish for three days and three nights; the walls of Jericho came tumbling down when his people shouted and the trumpets blared; the sun and the moon stood still in the heavens at the command of Joshua; Daniel spent a night unharmed in a den of lions.

The die was also cast for the New Testament. It, too, was to be accepted as a sacred, inerrant Book of God. Christians were to believe as literal and historical truths the Virgin Birth, the nativity stories, the feeding of the multitudes with five loaves and two fish, the raising of Lazarus from the dead, the turning of water into wine, the miraculous healing of lepers, Jesus walking on water and stilling the angry waves, and the physical resurrection of Jesus. Thus, by the fourth century the stage was set for centuries of conflict between faith and reason, scripture and science.

CHAPTER 8

Early Christian Texts

As a 16-year-old, I assumed that the books of the New Testament were based on original manuscripts. I was not told otherwise by any minister or teacher. Ministers and priests have studied the earliest Christian texts. They know we do not have a single original manuscript of any New Testament book, and that the oldest complete New Testaments only go back to the fourth century. From their seminarian studies, they know there are many differences in these early manuscripts, as well as the thousands of other manuscripts copied and translated in the following centuries. Unfortunately, clerics have not shared with us what they were taught in textual analysis. I have included this chapter to help fill this void of silence.

You likely have one or more Bibles in your home. No matter what version(s) you have, editors had to choose between different texts and different translations. Their goal was to print a Bible that was as free as possible from errors, and as close as possible to the early Greek and Latin manuscripts. This was a daunting task.

Before the invention of the printing press, it took many days of tedious copying to make a single copy of the New Testament. It was inevitable that there would be spelling and grammatical errors. Sometimes a bored or tired scribe would leave out a word or inadvertently skip a whole line. A scribe might substitute one word for another, thinking he was improving the text, or he might add a personal comment, called a gloss, in the margin. Years later, another scribe who liked the gloss, would add it to his manuscript. Other scribes tried to improve or correct the text by editing it. It is sometimes easy to spot such editing because a phrase or a word stands out in a different handwriting, or in a different colour of ink. Erasures are also obvious.

I am reminded of a story of a middle-aged monk cloistered for years in a tiny room copying and translating scripture. One day he enters the office of his abbot with a scroll in his hand and a look of utter dismay on his face. "Father, we've made a terrible mistake", he laments. "The word is celebrate, not celibate!"

In addition to examining early manuscripts, conscientious editors had to take into account thousands of scriptural fragments—some are from the second century. These fragments are very important. I will cite five of them. It is worth noting that none of these ancient fragments was written in Aramaic, the common language spoken by Jesus and his first disciples. They are all written in Greek.

1) **Papyrus 52,** also known as St. John's Fragment, was found in a trash pile in Upper Egypt. It was written, according to the estimates of paleographers—experts in ancient handwriting—in the year 125 CE, plus or minus 25 years. It contains five verses from the Gospel According to John (18:31-33, 37, 38) on a papyrus codex 3½ x 2½ inches. A codex is in book form; during the first four centuries of the Christian era, it replaced the bulkier, more fragile scrolls. Papyrus 52 was purchased in Egypt by Bernard Grenfell in 1960. It is preserved today in the John Ryland University in Manchester, U.K.

2) **Papyrus 45** (part of the Chester Beatty Library in Dublin, Ireland) was discovered in the late 1920's. Most scholars think it was written between 250 and 325 CE. It is heavily damaged. It contains a total of only 23 chapters from the four gospels. One of its verses is particularly interesting. In Mark 6:3 the people who have come out to hear Jesus ask, *Is this not the son of the carpenter* . . . In later texts, however, the wording is different. In my Revised Standard Version of the New Testament, Mark 6:3 reads as follows: *Is not this the carpenter, the son of Mary* . . . Was Jesus the son of a carpenter or a carpenter? Which source is correct—Papyrus 45 or later manuscripts? You might wish to check your Bible to see which "wording" the editors chose for Your Bible.

Origen was an early Church theologian and author.[19] In his work *Against Celsus (6:36)*, he corrects Celsus for mocking Jesus "as a mere carpenter". "Celsus is blind also to this, that in none of the Gospels current in the Churches is Jesus himself ever described as being a carpenter." If we believe Origen (185-254) and Papyrus 45, Jesus was the son of a carpenter, not a carpenter; later texts erred in calling Jesus a carpenter.

3) **Papyrus 46**. This codex was discovered in Cairo in 1930. It contains most of the Pauline epistles. Originally, scholars estimated that it had 104 pages. Of this total 18 pages front and back were lost. Of the remaining 86 pages, 56 are kept in the Chester Beattie Library in Dublin, and 30 pages are located at the University of Michigan. All of the pages have lost bottom lines due to deterioration. Based on linguistics, most modern scholars date this codex c. 200 CE (about 135 years after the Apostle Paul was martyred during the reign of the Roman Emperor Nero).

4, 5) **Papyrus 66 and 75 (The Papyrus Bodner)**. These important manuscripts were discovered in 1952 near Dishna, Egypt, and subsequently purchased by Martin Bodner. Papyrus 66 is dated c. 200 CE and contains most of John's Gospel. Papyrus 75 is dated as an early third century manuscript; originally it was 144 pages in length. The 102 pages that survived contain approximately half of the texts of John and Luke. Neither of these early texts records the story of Jesus and the woman caught in adultery! The earliest manuscript to add this story is that of Codex Bezae, a fourth century Greek manuscript. You may be curious about your Bible. Did the editors of your Bible include this story? If they did you will find it in John 7:53 to 8:1-11.

The Latin Vulgate. By the end of the fourth century, there were numerous Latin manuscripts of bibles in existence. There were so many, and they differed so much from each other that in 382 CE, Pope Damascus commissioned St. Jerome to produce a revised Latin Bible. Jerome did so, relying on both Latin and Greek manuscripts. It is interesting to note that there are two verses in the Vulgate that are often quoted to support the doctrine of the Trinity. These two verses are

---

[19]   See Addendum A—*Early Christian Authors (100 to 400 CE)*.

known as the Johannine Comma. Jerome reluctantly included them in the Vulgate.

> *There are three that bear witness in heaven: the Father, the*
> *Word and the Spirit, and these three are one; and there are three*
> *that bear witness on earth, the Spirit, the water, and the blood,*
> *and these three are one* (1 John 5:7-8). The "Word" refers to
> Jesus; i.e. *and the Word became flesh and dwelt among us* (1:14).

I should point out that John Wycliffe and his associates translated the New Testament Latin Vulgate into English in the 1380's. Wycliffe was an Oxford professor, scholar, theologian, and preacher. It was a rebellious undertaking because the hierarchy of the Roman Catholic Church had forbidden the Bible to be translated into the commonly used language of the people. The masses, it was argued, needed the expertise of their priests to understand scripture. Consequently, only Greek or Latin translations of the Bible were approved by Rome for the English Christians. Wycliffe further alienated himself from Rome by preaching that Holy Scripture should be the primary authority for Christians. It is not surprising then that in 1415, the Council of Constance declared Wycliffe to be a heretic. But what is astounding is that Pope Martin V ordered all his books to be burned, his remains exhumed and burned, and his ashes cast into the Swift River!

Codex Vaticanus. This fourth century manuscript is one of the best and oldest Greek manuscripts we have of the New Testament. As with other early Greek manuscripts, it flows continuously, with no separation between words and very little punctuation. Where it originated is unknown, but many scholars speculate that it was first written in Egypt. It has been stored in the Vatican Library since the 15th century.

Codex Sinaiticus, also dated from the fourth century, was found in Egypt in 1859 by archaeologist Constantine von Tischendorf in the St. Catherine's convent at the base of Mount Sinai. It was a great discovery. Here, in an isolated religious community, he found a meticulously written, complete Greek manuscript of the New Testament, as well as two additional early, Christian texts—*The Shepherd of Hermas* and the

Epistle of Barnabas. Codex Sinaiticus, currently stored in the British Library, rivals the importance of Codex Vaticanus.

Common Omissions in both Vaticanus and Sinaiticus.

The omissions may surprise you. In neither codex do we find the story of the stoning of the woman guilty of adultery. In their account of The Lord's prayer we do not find the words . . . *but deliver us from evil.* Nor does Jesus say to his executioners, *Father forgive them; for they know not what they do.* (Luke 23:24) But the most startling omission occurs in the last chapter of Mark. His gospel ends at 16:8. *And they went out and fled from the tomb; for trembling and astonishment had come upon them; and they said nothing to any one, for they were afraid.*

Other fifth century texts add what is known as "the shorter ending". *But they reported briefly to Peter and those with him all that they had been told. And after this, Jesus himself sent out by means of them, from east to west, the sacred and imperishable proclamation of eternal salvation.* This ending is found in Codex Bobbiensis, early Syriac manuscripts, and well over a 100 hundred Armenian manuscripts written from 411 to 450 CE.

To further complicate the issue, later manuscripts add "the longer ending", an additional twelve verses describing the resurrection appearances to Mary Magdalene and his disciples, and Jesus' promise that those who believe will cast out demons, speak in tongues, pick up serpents, and heal the sick by the laying on of hands.

This longer ending is indeed strange! The writing style is different, and some of the Greek words and phrases in the disputed 12 verses are not typical of the rest of Mark. No other gospel includes the "signs" found here that believers will speak in new tongues, pick up serpents and drink deadly potions. Most textual scholars think these 12 verses were added to the original gospel. Their analyses, and the fact that the longer ending is not found in our two oldest codices, have convinced most editors to leave it out of their biblical editions. Unfortunately, this decision came too late for Christians who, even to this day, try to prove their faith by handling deadly rattlesnakes.

There are many other differences between Codices Vaticanus and Sinaiticus. John Burgon (1813-1888), Dean of Chichester Cathedral (U.K.), did a detailed comparison of these manuscripts, and found so many textual variances that he wrote, *It is in fact easier to find two consecutive verses in which these two manuscripts differ the one from the other, than two consecutive verses in which they agree* (See *Revision Revised* page 12 published in 1883). It is an ironic comment since it came from one who believed in the inerrancy of Holy Scripture! He is reputed to have said, *Either, with the best and wisest of all ages, you must believe the whole of Holy Scripture; or, with the narrow-minded infidel, you must disbelieve the whole. There is no middle course open to you.* [20]

Concluding Observations

In examining the aforementioned manuscripts, textual experts have found thousands of variances. Professor Bart Ehrman states it very bluntly. "There are more differences among our manuscripts than there are words in the New Testament".[21] Differences were obvious even in the early centuries of the Christian era. Origen (185-254), a Church Father and author, made the following complaint in his "Commentary on Matthew".

> *The differences among the manuscripts have become great, either from the negligence of some copyist or through the perverse audacity of others; they either neglect to check over what they have transcribed, or in the process of checking, they make additions or deletions as they please.* (15:14)

It is fair to say that modern biblical scholars, including evangelical fundamentalists, are in agreement that in copying and translating the Bible, scribes made thousands of errors. Conservative scholars tend to downplay these differences as inconsequential copying errors, minor spelling mistakes, grammatical mistakes, and misplaced words. Are they trivial errors? Is it a minor "variance" to add a story about Jesus not

---

[20] Another British scholar, Hermon Hoskier (1864-1938), made a similar study and found 3,036 textual variations, just in the four gospels. (See *Codex B and Its Allies*, by Bernard Quaritch)

[21] Ehrman, Bart D. *Misquoting Jesus: The Story Behind Who Changed the Bible and Why.* New York: HarperCollins, 2005, page10.

found in the earliest manuscripts—such as the story of the woman guilty of adultery?

Bart Ehrman, Chairman of Religious Studies at the University of North Carolina, began his biblical studies at Moody Bible College at the age of 18. At that point in his life, he believed in the inerrancy of the Bible as the "Word of God". As he studied the Gospel of Mark, he discovered a disturbing problem. In Mark 2:36, Jesus reminded the Pharisees of a story about King David entering the Jerusalem Temple when Abiathur was high priest. Jesus was referring to a passage of scripture found in 1Samuel 21:1-6. When Ehrman looked up this Old Testament passage, he discovered that David entered the Temple when Ahimelech was the High priest—not his son Abiathur. Try as he could to explain the discrepancy, he eventually came to the conclusion that either Mark had made a mistake or Jesus had. Either way it meant that the Bible was not the inerrant "Word of God". To Ehrman this error was far from trivial.

Other differences are important because they show the subjectivity of scribes and editors. My copy of Mark 1:41 reads as follows: *Moved with pity, he stretched out his hand* . . . but in Codex Bezae (5th century) and three other early Latin manuscripts, we find *Moved with anger*. Was Jesus moved with pity or anger? It is highly unlikely that a scribe would confuse a word like "anger" with "pity". So a scribe must have decided to change the words. Perhaps he did not think it right to describe Jesus as being moved with anger. There is a similar instance in Matthew 8:2-4 and Luke 5:12-16. Here, Matthew and Luke repeat the story told by Mark (1:40-44) about a leper coming to Jesus, begging to be healed. Matthew and Luke use almost the exact wording of Mark, except that in Mark, Jesus "sternly charged" the man after he heals him. Matthew and Luke, however, omit the words "sternly charged".

It seems clear that Matthew and Luke were uncomfortable citing stories that showed Jesus as being stern or angry. They preferred a compassionate Jesus. Thus, by "omission" they modified the text. Again I am reminded of Albert Schweitzer's observation that everyone has his or her own Jesus.

As a 16-year-old I believed that the New Testament was the inerrant, inspired word of God. By the time I was 20 I was struggling to make sense of the differences, errors, and editorial deletions and additions that I have described. In my first year of theology, I resolved this problem by deciding that the Bible, while not entirely the Word of God, **contained** the Word of God. This "solution" created a new dilemma. How would I decide which parts of scripture were the Word of God, and which parts were not? What would be my criteria? Eventually, I simplified matters by accepting the New Testament as a collection of books written by men.

In this chapter I have only summarized early Christian texts that were copied by hand. After the invention of the printing press, there was a plethora of new translations of bibles. In **Addendum B**, I have summarized major biblical editions from 1516 to 1881. These editions are important, because they are the templates of today's bibles. Some Christians contend that the King James Version of the Bible is the best edition thanks to editors who were inspired by God. If you read Addendum B, you will discover why The King James Version is no longer the Bible of choice for most churches.

CHAPTER 9

Divisive Church Splits of 451, 1054, and 1517

What we believe often depends on the particular church our parents attended. But did our parents really "choose" their denomination or did historical events—over which they had little or no control—influence their choice? In this chapter I will examine three major church schisms that were instrumental in determining the faith of many future generations of Christians.

The Schism of 451 (The Council of Chalcedon)

Leo I, Bishop of Rome, convened an ecumenical council of over 500 bishops, from the east and the west of the Roman Empire, in 451 CE. Its main purpose was to resolve a theological dispute over the nature of Christ. Some eastern bishops, such as Eutyches, taught that Christ had only one nature. They argued that the divinity and humanity of Christ were united as one. Other bishops, particularly those from the west, contended that Jesus was both fully divine and fully human—two natures in one person. It was a contentious issue. The Patriarchs of Alexandria, Antioch and Jerusalem refused to accept the ruling of the council that there were "two natures" in Christ, and went their own separate ways. Those who became independent from the Roman Catholic Church included the Ethiopian Orthodox Church, the Coptic Orthodox Church of Alexandrian, and the Armenian Orthodox Church.

The Council of Chalcedon also passed 28 canons (rules) pertaining to church authority and administration. The last canon gave the Episcopal Jurisdiction (or See) of Constantinople honour and authority second only to that of the See of Rome. When Leo I, Bishop of Rome, learned of these canons, he approved all of them except the 28th which he declared to be null and void. The issue of "leadership" was a bone of contention.

The Great East-West Schism of 1054

Emperor Constantine built his new imperial residence in 330 CE at Byzantium, naming it "Nova Roma" and later Constantinople. At that point in time, the two foremost centres of Christianity were Rome and Alexandria. That was soon to change. As Constantinople grew in size and importance as the eastern capital of the Roman Empire, the status of the Patriarch of Constantinople, Michael Caerularius, soon rivalled that of the See of Rome. Although both leaders claimed to have apostolic authority to lead their districts, the Roman Pontiff claimed to be the successor to Peter with divine authority to rule over the entire church. This claim created intense religious and political rivalry between these two Christian centres. The dispute was "resolved" by the Second Church Council of Constantinople in 381 CE. This council, presided over by the Bishop of Rome, declared the Patriarch of Constantinople to be the highest ranking bishop of the East with primacy next to the Pope.

The eastern churches under the jurisdiction of the Patriarch of Constantinople rejected this "ranking", and for the next 673 years, refused to acknowledge the Roman Pontiff as the supreme head of the Church. Matters came to a head in 1054 when Pope Leo IX sent Cardinal Humbert to Constantinople to persuade the Patriarch, Michael Caerularius, to acknowledge the supremacy of the Roman Pontiff. When the Patriarch refused to do so, he was excommunicated by Pope Leo IX! The Patriarch was not amused. He in turn excommunicated Cardinal Humbert! As a result of this acrimonious stalemate, the State Church of the Roman Empire split into two main branches—the Eastern Greek branch (including the Russian Orthodox Church), and the Western Latin branch.

The resulting enmity contributed to two horrendous acts of genocide at Constantinople. In 1182, sixty thousand Roman Catholic merchants and their families either fled or died in "The Massacre of the Latins". Four thousand survivors were sold as slaves to the Turks. Twenty-two years later, armies from the Fourth Crusade left Venice. They were supposed to sail to Egypt to attack the Muslim forces that controlled the Holy Land. Instead, they went to Constantinople. There they captured, sacked and looted this very wealthy city. Many inhabitants were raped and slaughtered. Along with large areas of the city, the great library of Constantinople was destroyed by fire. This attack by the "Latin Christians" on Constantinople, the Capital of the Byzantine Empire, was like a dagger to the heart of the Eastern Orthodox Churches. The East-West Schism was now almost irreconcilable.

The Great Schism of the 16th Century

In 1517, Martin Luther, an Augustinian monk, posted 95 theses on the Castle Church door in the university town of Wittenberg, Germany. It was a common practice of the day—a basis for debate. I have included 11 of Luther's theses in **Addendum C** so that you can appreciate why Pope Leo X was so angry with Luther. Many of Luther's theses dealt critically with the selling of indulgences. In Catholic theology, an indulgence is the full or partial remission of punishment for sins. It is granted by a priest after the sinner has confessed and received pardon. Indulgences could also be obtained on behalf of a deceased loved one to lessen time of punishment in purgatory. Today, the term "indulgences" is understood by Roman Catholics as a medieval practice of the past.

Pope Leo X (1475-1521) had renewed this tradition in order to raise money for the massive, expensive construction of St. Peter's Basilica in Rome. Some churches, using the printing press, had even mass-produced documents promoting indulgences. To Luther the selling of indulgences was tantamount to selling salvation, and contrary to biblical teachings. Luther held that human beings could be saved by faith alone *(sola fides)*, and not by donations to the Church. In the 86th thesis, he asked why the pope would not use his own considerable wealth to build the Basilica.

Luther sent a copy of his theses to his bishop, who in turn forwarded them to Rome. Pope Leo X's response came three years later on June

15, 1520, in his papal letter, Exerge Domini. *We condemn, reprove, and entirely reject each one and all of the aforementioned articles or errors.* There was to be no debate. Luther had crossed the line by challenging the doctrines of the church and the authority of the pope. His suggestion that the Pope use his own money to build St. Peter's Basilica, was not appreciated. He was declared a heretic and excommunicated.

There was a domino effect. Religious leaders such as H. Zwingli in Switzerland, John Calvin in France, and John Knox in Scotland also advocated scripture as the basis for faith and doctrine. As a result of this 16th century schism, major Protestant groups emerged including the Lutherans, Reformists, and Anabaptists.

Just as there were disagreements over apostolic succession and leadership, so there were differences among the "protesters". The emerging churches disagreed on interpreting scripture, doctrines, and practices. The result was a proliferation of Protestant churches. I was reminded of that reality one day as my wife, Lois, and I drove through a little town in North Dakota that had numerous churches. One was named The Church of God, a second was named The True Church of God, and a third called itself The Only True Church of God.

Concluding Thoughts

Many of us were pressured to follow "the Faith of our Fathers" by parents, peers, teachers, and clerics. My first girl friend was a charming 15-year-old girl I met swimming at a nearby weir. She was a Roman Catholic. It made no difference to me. She looked great in her bathing suit. At any rate when I told my mother she was a Roman Catholic, she told me not to see her anymore, and her mother gave her the same order when she learned I was a Protestant. So we met on a bridge close to her home, and continued our Saturday night dates until the romance petered out.

Our son married a Roman Catholic. We enjoyed meeting our new daughter-in-law and the wedding events. The night before the nuptials I shared a bottle of whiskey with the bride's father. He learned from me why I had left the ministry and I learned from him why he no longer attended Mass. What we had in common was immensely important. We both loved our "kids", and hoped they would have a long and happy life together. I vaguely remember finding my way back to a hotel room.

I think what I am trying to say by these anecdotes, is that people are no longer passive followers of the beliefs and religious customs of their ancestors. I suspect education has a lot to do with it. The more education people have, the more likely they are to think rationally and critically—to question what others tell them is right or wrong, particularly when the supernatural is added to the equation. Today many young and old are using the microscope of reason and history when they think about "the Faith of our Fathers."

CHAPTER 10

The Authority of the Apostolic Church

We saw in chapter seven that we have no original texts, and that those we do have, are rife with errors and differences. This raises a troubling question. How can we have confidence in the trustworthiness of the New Testament? This is a question that few Christians would have raised in the first 14 centuries, because most Christians were illiterate, and of those who were educated, few would have known of the textual problems I have outlined. Those who did question the reliability of scripture were given a standard answer—that Christ had passed on his authority to the apostles, and they in turn had passed on their authority to the bishops, presbyters and elders. In other words, Christians were to trust the authority of the apostolic church—the appointed leaders of the church for doctrine, scriptural interpretation, and morals.

Roman Catholics would say that this introductory paragraph is incomplete and misleading. They would likely revise my introduction by adding that Jesus chose the apostle Peter to lead his church, and that Peter passed on his leadership to the bishop of Rome. As proof, they would quote what Jesus said to Peter as recorded in Matthew 16:18.

And I tell you, you are Peter, and on this rock I will build
my church, and the powers of death shall not prevail against it.

It is a weak scriptural argument for the following reasons. Firstly, scholars are certain that the apostle Matthew did not write this gospel[22]. Secondly, only the author of Matthew recorded this verse. It is not found in the gospels of Luke, Mark, and John. Thirdly, the Christian who had the most influence in spreading Christianity in the first century was the apostle Paul. If Jesus had given special authority to Peter and the future bishop(s) of Rome, surely Paul would have mentioned this in at least one of his epistles to the early church communities. Fourthly, it is significant to notice that in Galatians Chapter two, Paul criticizes and corrects Peter over the issue of circumcision.

Did Jesus authorize Peter to pass on his leadership to the bishop of Rome? If so, there should be clear evidence in early church history. That, however, is not the case. If you look up the names of the "popes" listed by the Roman Catholic Church in the first 300 years of the Christian era, you will be reading the names of obscure bishops about whom we know little. For the first three centuries, the most influential Christian leaders were Justin Martyr of Samaria (100-165), Bishop Iranaeus of Lyons France (120-200), Clement of Alexandria (150-215) and Origen (185-254) of Alexandria. It is important to note that these early Christians leaders (in matters of doctrine and church practices) never consulted the bishops of Rome. Nor did they acknowledge that the bishop(s) of Rome had been given the mantle of leadership for the Holy Catholic Church.

If the bishop of Rome was the divinely appointed successor of Peter, it should have been evident at the first major Christian council that took place in 325 CE in Turkey, at Nicea. It was an ecumenical council with over 250 bishops in attendance. It was an important gathering. Its main purpose was to establish a consensus over the deity of Christ. The council also decided on a uniform date for the celebration of Easter, and passed 20 church canons (laws).

When I read the records of the Council of Nicaea, I found that no special prominence was given to the two priests who were sent to represent Sylvester I, the Bishop of Rome, who did not even attend. In fact, the sixth canon placed the bishops of Alexandria, Rome and Antioch on an equal footing.

---

[22]   See chapter 1, *Who Wrote the New Testament Gospels?*

> *Let the ancient customs in* Egypt, Libya, and Pentapolis
> *prevail: that the Bishop of Alexandria have jurisdiction in all*
> *these, since the like is customary for the Bishop of* Rome *also.*
> *Likewise in Antioch and the other provinces, let the Churches*
> *retain their privileges . . .*

One important issue was not on the agenda of the Council of
Nicaea—which Christian texts were sacred and which were heretical?
We know that by the fourth century, there were over 20 gospels in
circulation. If the bishop of Rome was the highest authority in the
Church, God's voice on matters of faith and doctrine, then he should
have been at the forefront determining which texts belonged in the
canon of the New Testament. But he wasn't. In 367 CE, Athanasius, the
Bishop of Alexandria, in his 39th Festal Letter to Egyptian congregations,
listed 27 texts he pronounced to be authentic and sacred. He wrote, *Let
no one add anything to them or take anything away from them.*[23] If the
bishop of Rome was acknowledged as the head of the Christian Church,
why would Athanasius usurp the Pope's authority and decide which
books were sacred?

The Roman emperor, Constantine I, became a Christian in 312. In
the following year, he passed the Edict of Milan to end the persecution of
Christians. For the Christian communities in Rome it meant the dawn
of a new era of growth, influence and ambition. Rome at that point was
the capital of the Roman Empire; so it is not surprising that the bishops
of Rome would have political ambitions to lead a religion that was on
the fast track of becoming the state religion. This ambition was realized
in 380 CE when Christianity became the sole, official state religion of
the Roman Empire. In passing the Edict of Thessalonica[24], the Roman
emperors, Theodosius I, Gratian and Valentinian, made it clear to all
their subjects that the bishop of Rome was the pontiff—the head of the
Church. The edict reads as follows:

> *It is our desire that all the various nations which are subject*
> *to our Clemency and Moderations, should continue to profess that*

---

[23]   See Metzger, Bruce M. *The Canon of the New Testament.* Oxford,
       Clarendon, 1987 (pgs 213-214).
[24]   Codex *Theodosianus, xvi.1. 2.*

> *religion which was delivered to the Romans by the divine Apostle*
> *Peter, as it has been preserved by faithful tradition, and which*
> *is now professed by the Pontiff Damasus and by Peter, Bishop of*
> *Alexandria, a man of apostolic holiness.*

This elevation of the bishop of Rome to that of pontiff of the Universal Catholic Church was a bone of contention as noted in chapter 9—*Divisive Church Splits: 451, 1054, and 1517.*

CHAPTER 11

The Eastern Crusades (1095-1270)

You may be wondering why I have included a chapter and an addendum on the Crusades. What has this to do with *"The Faith of Our Fathers" Under the Microscope of Reason and History*? I have done so a number of reasons. I thought it important to highlight the political power wielded by Roman Catholic popes over kings and nations in medieval times. I wanted my readers to know that popes were responsible for initiating six Crusades! The Crusaders wore the sign of the Cross on their tunics, but that did not stop them from raping, slaughtering, robbing, and vandalizing the inhabitants and defenders of the cities they sacked. It is a black chapter of church history that we should not forget.

I also wanted to show the anti-Semitism unleashed by the Crusades. For example in the third Crusade, as the army passed by Jewish communities in France and Germany, mayhem frequently occurred. Jews were beaten and robbed; others were murdered as "killers of Christ". These crimes were chronicled by witnesses such as Ekkehard of Aura, Albert of Aiy, and Solomon bar Simson. Medieval historians Robert E. Lerner (professor emeritus at Northwestern University) and Thomas Asbridge (University of London scholar) also chronicled the crimes committed against the Jews at Cologne, Mainz, Trian, Metjz, and the Rhineland.

Although these violent attacks were condemned by the Roman Catholic Church, it is sad that popes and church councils did little to repudiate the popular notion that Jews were to blame for the crucifixion.

It was not until 1965—seven centuries after the last Crusade—that the Second Vatican Council issued the document, *Nostra Aetate*. It stated that Christ's death could not be attributed to Jews as a whole. It is unfortunate that the council's message was not understood by Mel Gibson, director and writer of the 2004 movie, *The Passion of the Christ*.

In 2011, Pope Benedict XVI made it very clear that Jews were innocent of the death of Jesus Christ. In his book, *Jesus of Nazareth Part 2*, he analyzed each gospel's account of Jesus' final hours. He concluded that it was "the temple aristocracy" and a few supporters of Barabbas who clamoured for Jesus to be put to death, and not the Jewish people. Unfortunately, the message of the Second Vatican Council, and that of Pope Benedict XVI, came centuries too late for the Jewish victims of the Crusades.

Lastly, I thought it important to show that the sacking and burning of Constantinople (in the fourth Crusade) had dire consequences. Firstly, it greatly weakened the Byzantine Empire and, consequently, contributed to the fall of Constantinople to the Ottoman Turks in 1453. Secondly, the attack on Constantinople effectively dashed any hopes for reconciliation between the western and eastern churches. It took almost 13 centuries before a Latin pope would come in a spirit of peace and reconciliation to meet with the leaders of the Eastern Orthodox Churches. In 2001, Pope John Paul II travelled to Greece to meet Archbishop Christodoulou. To the applause of the Archbishop and the Orthodox clergy, John Paul gave a sweeping apology expressing profound regret "for the sins of action and omission" against Orthodox Greek Christians.

The cost of the Crusades in terms of human life was considerable. The editors of *The Twentieth Century Atlas* attempted to determine the number of fatalities by listing the varying estimates of 12 historians, and came up with a median figure of between three and four million deaths. This number included those who perished in battle, or later from their wounds, the combatants who died from illnesses and starvation, and the civilian populations who died in the attacks on their communities.

What did the Crusades accomplish? The Holy Land remained under Islamic control. Christians who undertook a pilgrimage to Jerusalem did so at great, personal risk. Relations between eastern and western Christians reached a new low. As I pondered how to conclude this chapter, I remembered the following statement by Steven Weinberg[25], a Nobel prize-winning physicist. It seems to apply rather well.

> *With or without religion, good people will do good, and evil people will do evil. But for good people to do evil, that takes religion.*

It is customary to describe the Holy Land Crusades as eight in number. For those interested in the historical details, I have added **Addendum D** to summarize the campaigns. I have also included the papal decrees that initiated the Crusades.

1. Initiated by Pope Urban II, *1095-1110,* at the Council of Clermont.
2. Initiated by Pope Eugene III, 1145-47, by his bull *Quantum praedecessores.*
3. Initiated by Pope Gregory VIII, *1188-92,* in his bull *Audita tremendi.*
4. Initiated by Pope Innocent III, 1202-04, through his sermons.
5. Initiated by Pope Innocent III, 1213-21, in his Encyclical, Quia maior.
6. Initiated by Emperor Frederick II and Pope Gregory IX, *1228-29.*
7. Initiated by King Louis IX, 1248-50.
8. Initiated by King Louis IX, 1270.

25   From a speech given on April of 1999 at Washington D.C. at the Conference for the American Association for the Advancement of Science.

CHAPTER 12

Decrees of the Roman Pontiffs

In this chapter I examine eight decrees of Roman popes. You probably are aware of a few of them, but some of them may shock you. These papal decrees are often referred to as encyclicals and bulls. If you are interested in the exact wording of these edicts, see **Addendum E.**

1—Decrees Pertaining to Salvation

Pope Innocent III, at the Fourth Lateran Council of 1215, stated that there was only one universal church whereby the faithful could be saved. Pope Boniface VIII, in 1302, added another prerequisite that had implications for Eastern Orthodox Christians—you had to be subject to the Roman Pontiff. In 1441, Pope Eugene IV issued a bull that decreed that only those within the Roman Catholic Church would go to heaven. All others were doomed for an eternity in hell.

In the succeeding centuries many Roman Catholics have been troubled and embarrassed by the exclusive stance of these medieval popes. Surely God would not exclude and punish devout members of Protestant churches, as well as members of the Eastern Orthodox Church? Would God also exclude the infants and children of Muslims, Hindus and Buddhists? Would they, too, go to hell?

To the best of my knowledge, these questions were not formally addressed until the Second Vatican Council, convened by Pope John

Paul VI in 1962. This council in its document, *Lumen Gentium,* acknowledged that there were Christians outside the Roman Catholic Church. This was a profound change from an exclusive position to one of respectful inclusion. Today, we can say without equivocation, that popes no longer endorse the exclusive conditions for salvation announced by Pope Innocent III, Pope Boniface VIII, and Pope Eugene IV.

2—Decrees Pertaining to the Inquisition

In 1184, Pope Lucius III laid the groundwork for centuries of persecution when he decreed that all heretics, and their followers, were to be excommunicated. He decreed that if those accused could not prove their innocence, or if they refused to repent of their heretical views, they were to be handed over to the civil authorities for punishment. Heretics were to lose their right to hold public office, the right to trial, the right to make a will, and the right to inherit land or positions. Patriarchs, archbishops and bishops were to lose their church positions if they failed to actively seek out heretics, and follow the prescribed measures.

In 1231, the Inquisition officially began when Pope Gregory IX appointed special, permanent judges (inquisitors) to act on his behalf to find, try, and sentence heretics. The church, through its popes and councils, was responsible for determining which beliefs were acceptable (orthodox) and which beliefs were false (heresy). If the guilty refused to confess their errors and repent, they were excommunicated. Some were handed over to civil authorities for further punishment. When the inquisitors handed over unrepentant heretics to the civil authorities, they were in effect condoning whatever punishments the civil authorities decreed—fines, imprisonment, torture or execution.

Pope Innocent IV gave new powers to the inquisitors. In 1252, he issued his infamous *Ad Extirpanda,* a decree that allowed the State to confiscate property of convicted heretics. This decree described heretics as "murderers of souls as well as robbers of God's sacraments and of the Christian faith". The bull authorized inquisitors to "coerce" heretics into confessing their errors of doctrine, but there were specific restrictions. In their "interrogations", inquisitors were not to cause loss of life or limb!

One of the methods sanctioned by inquisitors was known as the "strappado". The accused was suspended from the ceiling by the wrists, which were tied behind the back. Sometimes weights were tied to the ankles. The suspending ropes could be jerked up and down, to increase the pressure on the shoulders. In addition to the rack, another tactic of "coercion" was that of water boarding—pouring water over a cloth covering the face of a bound victim. Those who confessed their errors of belief could be given penances, such as a pilgrimage, a public whipping, or a fine. Those who did not recant could be imprisoned, tortured indefinitely, or executed.

Some states were very lenient, while others (particularly those of Spain and South America) were guilty of ruthless persecution. In 1492, Spanish Jews were given the choice of becoming Catholics or leaving the country. The Spanish inquisitors sought out the Jews who had publicly converted to Catholicism, but who, in private, still practised Judaism. In 1691, at Palma, 37 Jews were put to death in public spectacles. After being garrotted, 34 were burned in bonfires. Three were burned alive.

A few years ago, my wife and I visited the Museum of the Inquisition in Lima, Peru. It was used as a torture chamber for over two hundred years, from 1570 to 1820. We walked down the steps to the basement, and through the dimly lit rooms that displayed the various instruments of "coercion". On each side of these larger rooms were tiny, cramped dungeon cells. It was a quiet, eerie experience. You can still visit the museum, located on the Plaza Bolivar.

Modern historians are cautious in estimating how many people were executed during the Inquisition. Too many records have been lost or burned. We do know, however, from existing court records, that of those accused, few were actually found guilty, and even fewer were put to death. For example, in the 15 years of Bernard Gui's administration, this famous French inquisitor (also Bishop of Lodeve) found over 900 persons guilty of heresy or blasphemy, but of this number only 42 were executed by civil authorities. Those executed were usually unrepentant and had expressed their unorthodox views by their speeches or writings.

Allow me to cite one example—that of Giordano Bruno. He was an Italian Dominican friar, philosopher, author, mathematician, and astronomer. The Inquisition found him guilty of pantheism.[26] They also objected to his ideas about astronomy. While the Roman Catholic

---

[26] For the pantheist, God is an impersonal presence and power found everywhere in nature, as well as the cosmos.

Church taught that the earth was at the centre of the universe, Bruno, like Copernicus, thought that planets and stars revolved around the sun. Centuries ahead of his peers, he taught that in the infinite number of planets, some were likely to support intelligent life. The Roman Inquisition found him guilty of heresy and turned him over to the civil authorities. On February 17, 1600, he was burned to death at the stake, together with his books.

Popes Lucius III, Gregory IX, and Sixtus IV, initiated over six hundred years of injustice, violence, and death. Although the editors of the Catholic Encyclopedia try to rationalize and minimize their church's involvement and responsibility in the Inquisition, Pope John Paul II did not. In 2004, he issued a formal apology to Jews, Galileo, and other victims of the Inquisition. He called the Inquisition "the greatest error in Church history."

3—Decrees Pertaining to Witches

In 1484, Pope Innocent VIII issued a decree that was used by many witch-hunters to justify their condemnation, persecution, torture, and execution of witches. If you read this decree in Addendum E, there are two terms you may not be familiar with—incubi and succubi. The former refers to evil spirits or demons, said to have sexual intercourse with men in their sleep. The latter refers to demons or evil spirits said to have sexual intercourse with women in their sleep. Be wary. After reading *Summis Desiderantes Affectibus,* you might have insomnia.

Three years later Kramer and Sprenger, members of the Dominican Order, and inquisitors for the Roman Catholic Church, wrote *Malleus Maleficarum* (the Hammer of Witches). In their book they listed reasons for believing in the existence of witchcraft, and then described the various forms of witchcraft. The last chapters were for magistrates—to help them to confront and combat witchcraft. Published twenty-nine times, it was a manual that systemized the persecution of witches. It was widely used by both Catholic and Protestant witch-hunters for the next two hundred years.

How many "witches" were hanged, strangled or burned at the stake? Modern historians now discount earlier estimates that are in the millions. For instance, Robin Biggs[27] summed up his research with these words:

> *On the wilder shores of the feminist and witch-cult movements a potent myth has become established, to the effect that 9 million women were burned as witches in Europe; gendercide rather than genocide. This is an overestimate by a factor of up to 200, for the most reasonable modern estimates suggest perhaps 100,000 trials between 1450 and 1750, with something between 40,000 and 50,000 executions, of which 20 to 25 per cent were men.*

Eventually, the witch-hunt spread to the puritan communities in North America. There were 162 trials at Salem, Massachusetts. Only those who were defiant were put to death. Even so, 19 women were hanged, and one man was pressed to death by heavy stones. To "google" the names and trials of those who died, type in "individuals executed in the Salem trials." I found the Salem trial records depressing and disturbing because of the "evidence" that convicted the accused—young women probably suffering from epilepsy or mental illness.

The accusations brought against "the witches" were incredible. Was your child stillborn? A witch must have cast an evil spell. Did your crops fail? Witches did it. Erectile dysfunction? A witch was responsible. When I think of the innocent victims condemned as witches, I am reminded of the observation made by Lucretius (c. 99-55 BCE) in his poem, *De rerum natura*. He wrote, *Tantum religio potuit suadere malorum* (To such heights of evil are men driven by religion).

Popes and bishops were not the only church leaders to believe in witches. Protestants, such as Luther and Calvin, also advocated the extermination of witches. When it came to belief in demons, incantations, spells, incubi and succubi, the religious leaders of this era were as superstitious as the average European.

---

[27] *Witches and Neighbours: the Social and Cultural Context of European Witchcraft*, New York Viking, 1996, 8.

4—Decrees Pertaining to the Colonization of the New World (1492-1898)

Most of us are familiar with the names of the most famous conquistadors—Hernán Cortés who conquered the Aztecs, and Francisco Pizarro who defeated the Incas. What we may not know is that their conquests were justified and encouraged by two popes. In 1492, Nicholas V issued a papal bull authorizing King Alfonzo V of Portugal to subjugate and enslave the defeated populations of the New World. In 1493, Alexander V issued a bull, *Inter Caetera,* that granted Spain all lands west and south of any of the islands of the Azores, or the Cape Verde Islands.

Citing apostolic authority to do so, Pope Alexander gave Spanish rulers full authority, not only to subjugate the "unbelievers", but also to "reduce their persons into perpetual slavery". It is astonishing—Popes Nicholas V and Alexander V believed that they had divine authority to give Portugal and Spain the right to conquer and colonize the New World discovered by Christopher Columbus.

The results were catastrophic for the indigenous peoples. They had neither the organization nor the weaponry to defeat mounted conquistadors with their armour, swords, and lances. Nor were they immune to the new diseases brought from Europe. Epidemics of smallpox, measles, influenza and diphtheria decimated their populations. H.F. Dobyns, a renowned American scholar, estimated that 95% of the total population of the New World died in the first one hundred and thirty years. According to the research of Cook and Borak of the University of Berkeley, the population in Mexico declined from 25.2 million in 1518 to 700,000 by 1623.

A harsh new economic system was imposed on the conquered peoples. Under the hacienda system (large land-holdings or plantations), land grants were given to the conquering conquistadors. The Franciscans, Dominicans, and Jesuits, were also granted vast hacienda holdings. For this system to work, the land owners required many labourers to work the land, raise the stock, or mine for minerals such as silver. The indigenous peoples who survived the wars and epidemics were forced to work the haciendas (along with millions of African slaves). My research into the colonization of the New World can be summed up by one word—depressing.

5—Decrees Pertaining to Martin Luther

After Pope Leo X condemned Martin Luther for posting his 95 theses, he gave Luther 60 days to retract 41 errors from his theses or face excommunication. When Luther failed to meet this deadline, Pope Leo X issued the bull, *Decet Romanum Pontificem.* By this decree he excommunicated Luther and all who supported him. It also called for the confiscation of all his property, and that of his descendants. In addition to the crime of heresy, Luther was declared to be guilty of treason.

Today, most religious leaders are respectful and courteous when discussing theological differences with other religious figures. So it is a little jarring to read of Pope Leo X describing Martin Luther as being depraved and damned. What might have happened if Leo X had invited Luther to Rome to debate his theses, or to help initiate long-overdue reforms? If you are interested in what Luther had to say in his famous theses, I have included 11 of them in **Addendum C.**

6—Decrees Pertaining to Jewish Italian Ghettoes

In 1555, Pope Paul IV issued a papal document that forced Jews into ghettos! By his infamous *Cum Minis Adsurdum,* the pope decreed that Jews living in urban centres should be segregated to live in only one area of Italian cities. Jewish homes were not to be located next to Christian homes. If you visit the city of Rome, check your tourist map to see if it shows an area of the city called the Jewish Ghetto. In the 16th century, it was a walled quarter with three massive gates that were closed each night. Jews were allowed to have but one synagogue; all others were destroyed. In order that Jews could be easily identified, men were required to wear yellow hats. They were forbidden to work on Sundays, or to fraternize with Christians. See Addendum E for a detailed list of the restrictions placed on Jews. It is a grim reminder of what happened to millions of Jews in Europe during World War II.

7—Decrees Pertaining to Papal Infallibility and the Assumption

In 1870 the First Vatican Council defined the Doctrine of Papal Infallibility. Although the Council recognized that no pope is free from sin or error, the council members decided that whenever the pope speaks *ex cathedra*[28] on matters of faith and morals, he is infallible. Catholics, who question or reject these divine proclamations, were to be denounced and excommunicated. This decree was contentious. When the bishops first debated it in 1870, a significant number opposed it on theological and historical grounds—88 bishops voted against it in the first round! Although the editors of the Catholic Encyclopaedia would have us believe that only two bishops cast dissenting votes, when I read the transcripts of this First Vatican Council, I discovered that there were 55 bishops who absented themselves at the final vote!

Although the Roman Catholic Church is reluctant to list the doctrines which must be accepted without debate or question, there are two papal dogmas decreed to be infallible—the Immaculate Conception of Mary and her Assumption (her bodily ascension into heaven).

In 1854, Pius IX in his proclamation *Ineffabilis Deus* stated that from the moment of her conception, Mary, the mother of Jesus, was preserved from all "stains of original sin". The original sin to which he referred is based on the biblical story of Adam and Eve in the Garden of Eden.[29] Here, they disobeyed God by eating of the fruit of the tree of knowledge of good and evil. Consequently, Adam and Eve were expelled from the Garden of Eden into a world where they would toil and labour to survive, and where they would endure pain and death. As a result of their disobedience, they transmitted their sin to all their descendants, and also the consequences of sin.

For centuries, this story of original sin posed a vexing dilemma for Roman Catholic theologians. If all mankind was tainted by the disobedience of Adam and Eve, then Mary must have been tainted, and if so, would she not have transferred the stain of original sin to her child, Jesus? In 1854 Pius IX answered this question by declaring that at

---

[28] This is a reference to those times the pontiff issues a formal definition of faith or morals "from the chair" of the Apostle Peter.

[29] See the Book of Genesis Chapter 3.

the very instance of her conception, she was free from original sin. This declaration, however, raised another problem. If Mary was not "tainted" by the sin of Adam and Eve, then what happened to Mary when she reached the end of her earthly life? Did she suffer the same fate as the rest of us—death? In 1950, Pope Pius XII resolved this quandary by his decree, *Munificentissimus Deus,* which we know as The Assumption. It stated that when Mary completed her earthly life, she immediately ascended to Heaven.[30]

Today, many Christians are uncomfortable with the belief that all of us, including newborn babies, are "stained by original sin". It does not make sense that a just and caring God would punish all of humanity for the disobedience of one couple, Adam and Eve. It seems unfair and unreasonable. Roman Catholics, however, are not supposed to ponder such thoughts. They are to believe that when the pope speaks *ex cathedra* on matters of faith and morals, he is infallibly expressing the will of God.

8—Decrees Pertaining to Birth Control

When Pope Paul VI issued his encyclical letter, *Humanae Vitae* in 1968, the only method of birth control approved by Roman Catholic popes and councils was "the Rhythm Method". The pope made it crystal clear that unlawful birth control methods were intrinsically wrong. It is also crystal clear that in Europe and North America, Roman Catholics continue to ignore this moral decree. Statistics show that Roman Catholics throughout the Western World have, on average, only one or two children. When it comes to birth control, many Roman Catholics make their own decisions.

This freedom of choice, however, does not apply to many third-world countries. Millions of people in Africa have scant knowledge of birth control methods and of sexually transmitted diseases. One sad consequence is that there are now millions of orphans in Africa who have lost one or both parents due to AIDS. How many of their parents died

---

[30]   Eastern Orthodox theologians believe that Mary experienced a physical death, as did Jesus, and that, similarly to Jesus, her body was raised from the dead three days later, and then taken up body and soul to heaven.

because they did not know about birth control methods? How many died because they could not afford condoms? How many died because they were told by priests that the use of condoms was a sin—forbidden by God?

Imagine for a few minutes that you are an Argentinean. Due to the economic downturn of 1991, you lost your job on a farm. Penniless and desperate you moved with your wife and two children to a suburb of Buenos Aires. Suburb is not quite the right word. You live in a shack you made by scrounging tin, wood and cardboard. The narrow dirt "street" outside your shack is rutted. There is no sewer infrastructure. When it rains your street becomes a cesspool. You do, however, have several electrical outlets because you "tapped" into a city hydro grid. You accept whatever menial work you can find. Your wife collects and sells cast-off clothing. You are living in a villa of misery.

You worry about your kids. They walk to a primary school eight blocks away—through an area that is a haven for thieves and drug dealers. Only half of your neighbours' teenagers go to high school. You lose sleep worrying about the health and future of your children.

You are grateful to your church and particularly to Cardinal Jorge Mario Bergoglia. You once met him and now he is the pope! Thanks to his example and influence there are a number of priests working in the slums of Buenos Aires. They do more than offer Mass on Sundays in chapels or soccer fields. They help provide food, clothing, youth organizations and drug rehabilitation programmes. They serve a large parish—half a million families live as you do.[31]

You are grateful to the priest assigned to your villa, but one thing he says greatly puzzles and distresses you. He forbids the use of condoms. To use them, he said, would be a sin against God. This is so hard to understand. Why would God want you to have more children when you are struggling to provide for just two children? And yet, he says it is a sin to use a condom.

---

[31] According to Merco Press (March of 2013) of the South Atlantic News Agency

CHAPTER 13

Creationism Vs Science

Four hundred years ago, our ancestors believed that God created the cosmos exactly as described in the first three chapters of the Bible, in Genesis. They believed God created the heavens and the earth and all its inhabitants in six days, and then rested on the seventh day.

When did all this happen? Archbishop James Ussher of Ireland (1581-1656) thought he could determine the exact date. By adding up all the generations outlined in the Bible from Adam to Jesus, he concluded that God began his first day of creation on Monday, October 23, 4004 BCE. If you add the years from the time of Jesus to the present time, you have a creation date that occurred approximately 6,000 years ago. According to some who take the Bible literally, that is when God created everything.

It may surprise you, but many North Americans believe that the story of creation in the Book of Genesis is true and scientifically accurate. According to the Canadian Press Decima Research, published July 3, 2007, 26% of Canadians believed God alone created humans 6,000 to 10,000 years ago. The American Gallup Poll, taken in December of 2010, showed that 40% of Americans believed in an instant creation that happened 6,000 to 10,000 years ago! The polls also showed that the level of education is a factor. University graduates are much less likely to believe in an instant creation than high school graduates.

But not always. My grandson had a Mormon friend who attended the University of Calgary. In his first year he chose an introductory course in geology. Raised to believe in an instant creation, he was puzzled and disturbed by his first semester classes; his professors presented a detailed, scientific explanation of the origin of the earth, and the eons of time represented by the various layers of rock that make up the earth's crust. Whom should he believe—his professors or his church? So he sought the counsel of a church elder. His elder had interesting explanations. He said that God had created the earth from huge rocks from the universe, and that inside some of these rocks were the skeletons of dinosaurs. My grandson's friend found a solution to his dilemma. He switched to a business programme.

Knowing this story, I was sceptical when someone told me that the foremost Mormon university, Brigham Young, accepts and teaches evolution. So I researched the university's website. In describing their biology major, I found these summarizing statements.

> *This major provides students with a current understanding of the full breadth of biology . . . This degree focuses on understanding the diversity of life, emphasizing whole organism biology in ecological and evolutionary contexts. In Bio 220 students study Clade Animalis Evolution. This course also covers Phylogenetic Systematics so that students will develop the skills necessary to understand . . . the methods used to recover 'the tree of life,' the logic behind the hierarchy (i.e. the only possible outcome of the process of 'descent with modification'), and critically apply evolutionary reasoning . . . to formulate and test hypotheses that explain biological diversity.*

Interesting! Mormon congregations and children are taught creationism (that there was an instant creation about 6,000 years ago), but at their premier university of Brigham Young, they are taught evolution!

Baylor University in Waco, Texas, is the largest Baptist University in the world. Do they teach creationism or evolution or both? If you use your computer to access their Department of Biology, you will find the following "Statement of Evolution."

> *Evolution, a foundational principle of modern biology, is supported by overwhelming scientific evidence and is accepted*

> *by the vast majority of scientists. Because it is fundamental to the understanding of modern biology, the faculty in the Biology Department at Baylor University, Waco, TX, teaches evolution throughout the biology curriculum. We are in accordance with the American Association for Advancement of Science's statement on evolution. We are a science department, so we do not teach alternative hypotheses or philosophically deduced theories that cannot be tested rigorously.*

If you're curious to know how scientists date not only the age of our universe and our planet earth, but also the age of ancient bones, parchments, and pieces of wood, I invite you to read **Addendum F**. Here I describe three important geological clocks—fossils and sedimentary rocks, radioactive decay, and carbon 14. In chapter 15, I examine the more sophisticated arguments of *Intelligent Design* versus E*volution*, but before doing so I would like to examine two stories from the Book of Genesis. Creationists believe that Genesis is the inspired Word of God and, therefore, is a reliable, accurate source for our knowledge of the planet Earth and God. Is it?

CHAPTER 14

The Book of Genesis

The Creation Stories: the Book of Genesis contains two creation stories.[32] As we examined the first story in my first year of theology, one of my classmates interrupted Professor Dobbie, our professor of the Old Testament. My classmate pointed out that in Genesis 1:3-5 God created light so that there was day and night. That was on the first day of creation. He asked our professor how it was possible to have "an evening" and a "morning" without a sun, which was created on the fourth day.

Secondly, he pointed out that while God created plants and trees on the third day, it wasn't until the fourth day that God created the sun. How could there be plant life without the sun? Without the sun's energy photosynthesis can't occur—a chemical process vital for plant life and for the oxygen in our atmosphere. Yet, according to Genesis, plant life of all kinds came into being on the third day, **before** the creation of the sun! My classmate asked our professor if he could explain these paradoxes.

Professor Dobbie was not one to be cornered by first year theologians. I don't remember his exact words but this is the gist of his answer. He said if one wanted to know **how** the earth came into being, one ought to ask scientists—geologists, astronomers, physicists, biologists and chemists. But if one wanted to know from whence came the energy that created the universe, then one should read the first four words of the Bible, *In the beginning God . . .*

---

[32] Genesis 1 to 2:3 and Genesis 2: 4-25.

Actually we could have pointed out a few more scientific problems. On the fourth day God created "the stars". It would have been a busy 24 hours indeed! Thanks to astronomers, like Edwin Hubble, we know that our Milky Way Galaxy is not the only one. There are billions of galaxies in our rapidly expanding universe, and yet, according to Genesis, God created them all in one day. You will note that all the stars were put there just for us—*he made the stars also. And God set them in the firmament of the heavens to give light upon the earth!* The exclamation mark is mine. Just imagine the enormity of it all—billions and billions of stars all created to help illuminate our tiny planet.

In the second creation account in Genesis 2:4-25, God creates man first, then the Garden of Eden with plants and trees, then the rivers, next the animals and birds, and lastly woman. I will leave it to you to decide if the order of events, the chronology, is in sync with what you have learned from the fossil records, and from the books and articles you have read on anthropology and biology.

The Theology of Creation

The God of Genesis is not omnipotent. He is fatigued after six days of creating and has to rest on the seventh. Nor is he all-knowing. It's not until he sees Adam and Eve trying to hide their nakedness that he realizes that they have eaten of the tree of the knowledge of good and evil. He did not see that happening?

The God of Genesis is very angry with Adam and Eve. He does not forgive them for eating of the fruit of the tree of knowledge. Apparently the merciful injunction of Jesus[33] that we are to forgive each other, not seven times, but seven times seventy, only applies to humans, and not to the Creator. So God expels them from the Garden of Eden. He announces some special punishments for Eve. *I will greatly multiply your pain in childbearing; in pain you shall bring forth children . . .* and your husband *shall rule over you (Genesis 3:16).* Because Adam listened to Eve, God curses the ground causing it to produce thorns and thistles. *In the sweat of your face you shall eat bread till you return to the ground for out of it you were taken (Genesis 3:19).* Here then is their final punishment.

---

[33]   Matthew 18: 21, 22.

Adam and Eve are now mortal beings who will someday die, and so will their children, and their children's children.

Death will come in many ways. In the world outside the Garden of Eden there will be parasites and hosts, predators and prey. There will be tuberculosis, malaria, typhoid, chicken pox, measles, diphtheria, hookworm parasites, viral pneumonia, leprosy and a plethora of cancers. A virulent bacteria called *Yersinia Pestis* will attack lymph glands. In the 14th century of the Christian era, this terrible plague will kill one-third of the population of China and Europe! Millions. Thus, according to the writer of Genesis, the disobedience of Adam and Eve, will have grave and deadly consequences for centuries. Billions will suffer because of the sin of one couple. This story, if accepted literally, makes God a heartless, vengeful deity. The irony is that Christians who believe Genesis to be "the Word of God" are still praying to God as, "Our Father". But Genesis has much more to say about the nature of God in the second story, and it is not positive.

The Story of Noah and the Ark (Chapters 6-9)

Nine generations after Adam, Noah was born. *Noah was a righteous man, blameless in his generation.* His generation was not. *The Lord saw that the wickedness of man was great in the earth.* Regretting that he had made man, the Lord said, *I will blot out man whom I have created from the face of the ground, man and beast and creeping things and birds of the air.*

But God decided to save eight people—Noah, his wife, their three sons and three daughters-in-law. God commanded Noah to build an ark. *And of every living thing of all flesh, you shall bring two of every sort into the ark, to keep them alive with you; they shall be male and female.* Obviously, God must have included pigs, camels and hares in this mandate. Yet later, in Leviticus 11:4-7, God declares these animals to be "unclean", and forbids the people of Israel to eat them. An omniscient Creator would have had the foresight to exclude them from the ark.

Noah obeyed. He built the ark and brought in two of every sort. Then it rained for forty days and nights.

And the waters prevailed so mightily upon the earth that all the high mountains under the whole heaven were covered . . .

and all flesh died that moved upon the earth . . . and the waters prevailed upon the earth 150 days.

When the water finally abated, the ark came to rest on a mountain. More time passed until finally the earth was dry and Noah set free his family and all the creatures. Then Noah built an alter and offered burnt offerings. This is amazing. Even though God had just wiped out all of humanity, except for one family, Noah's first thought on surviving the Flood is to worship God. Even though God was responsible for the deaths of millions of innocent, blameless children and animals, Noah wanted to please the Almighty. *And when the Lord smelled the pleasing odor, the Lord said in his heart, 'I will never again curse the ground because of man . . . neither will I ever again destroy every living creature as I have done'.* I wonder which animal(s) Noah selected for the burnt offerings. Perhaps it was a pair of unicorns?

Consider the size of the ark—300 cubits long, 50 cubits wide and 30 cubits high. A cubit is the distance from the elbow to the fingertips. It varied among ancient cultures from 17.5 to 20.6 inches long. If we take a cubit as being 20" long, then the ark was 500' long, 83' wide and 50' high (for 3 decks). Noah had to build this structure prior to the Bronze Age—before there were axes, saws, nails or steel. He had to make it waterproof using pitch on the inside and the outside. The building and waterproofing of the ark would have been a formidable and time-consuming task, even for a marine engineer with a trained crew of 100 carpenters. Noah only had his family—a total of eight persons.

Consider too the occupants of the ark. It had to accommodate all the animals, birds, and reptiles of the world—thousands and thousands of species. How did Noah catch and cage the birds? How did Noah locate and transport the animals indigenous only to Australia, Asia, Madagascar, South America, and the Galapagos Islands? What about the predators? Did Noah include two Sabre Tooth Tigers or two of Tyrannosaurus Rex—a dinosaur 40' long, 13' high, weighing over 7 tons?

Consider too the cargo of the ark. Noah would have needed a great deal of storage space for food and fresh water—enough to last the 200 days they lived in the ark. Many animals and birds require specific foods. Pandas, for example, eat twenty pounds of bamboo shoots each day. It is impossible to even imagine eight adults looking after this humongous cargo. Think of the noise, the lack of light, the lack of ventilation, and the smells! It is mindboggling.

There is also a problem with the amount of water needed to flood the earth. According to Genesis 7:20 all the mountain tops were covered with water. Our planet has more than 100 mountains over 20,000 feet in height. Yet according to Genesis, the Great Flood covered **all** the mountains. Where did the water come from? Even if all the glaciers melted during the 40 days of rain, there still would not be enough water to cover the mountains.

Some advocates of Genesis have a novel explanation. They argue that most of the water needed to cover the mountains came from the atmosphere. This argument ignores the thermodynamic principle of condensation; namely, that when a vapor turns into water, heat is created. Vast quantities of water would be required to cover the mountains. If most of this water came from atmospheric condensation, the heat released would have created a boiling sea of water in which nothing could survive.

Lastly, consider the consequences of water covering the earth for 200 days. Such an inundation would have killed all the trees and most plants. There would have been no "freshly plucked olive leaf" for a dove to find (8:11). There would have been no food for the animals released from the ark, and no food for Noah and his family.

The Theology of the Flood

Before I consider *The Theology of the Flood,* it is important to compare the Genesis story to a much earlier one known as the Sumerian flood myth. This story was discovered in 1853, at Nineveh, in *The Epic of Gilgamesh* written on clay tablet number eleven. It was carbon dated to c. 2500 BCE. In the third millennium BCE, there were 25 city states built on the fertile land between the Tigris and Euphrates Rivers in ancient Mesopotamia (Iraq and Syria). Floods occurred frequently, especially in the lower delta. The Sumerian legend of a huge flood probably originated from a devastating storm or a tidal wave, and the subsequent flooding that inundated many of the lower city states.

In this story, Enlil (air god), the chief divinity of the Sumerian gods, was so angry with man that he persuaded the gods to destroy humanity by a great flood. But the god Ea or Enki took pity on a virtuous man called Uta-Napishtim. He was told to build a huge boat so that he could save himself, his kin, and all the living things that he could load onto the six decks of his boat. Uta did as he was told. The walls were each ten times 12 cubits in height. With six decks, the boat was huge, like a field. *All the living beings that I had I loaded on it, I had all my kith and kin go up to the boat, all the beasts.* When the storm finally subsided after six days and seven nights, the boat was safely lodged on a mountain.

> *When a seventh day arrived I sent forth a dove and released it. The dove went off, but came back to me; I sent forth a swallow and released it. The swallow went off, but came back to me. I sent forth a raven and released it. The raven went off, and saw the waters slither back. It eats, it scratches, it bobs, but does not circle back to me. Then I sent out everything in all directions and sacrificed. I offered incense in front of the mountain-ziggurat. Seven and seven cult vessels I put in place . . . the gods smelled the sweet savor, and collected like flies over a (sheep) sacrifice.*

The similarities to Genesis are obvious. The God of Genesis is very similar to the unpredictable Sumerian gods who talk and walk and display human emotions. In the *Epic of Gilgamesh,* humans had good reason to be fearful of these powerful and capricious gods. The gods were responsible for whatever catastrophes happened. Therefore humans had to be both respectful and wary of the gods—placating them with sacrifices, pleasing odours, and rituals. The Flood hero, Uta-Napishtim, is a heroic symbol of man surviving even the wrath of the gods in a calamitous flood. As you can see, the two stories are similar in content and in theology.

Consider what the God of Genesis does in the flood story. God gives up on the human race, except for one family. He is so angry and vengeful that he kills all but eight people. He drowns innocent children, innocent animals, innocent birds and insects, and all the fauna, trees and flowers.

> *All things bright and beautiful,*
> *All creatures great and small,*
> *All things wise and wonderful,*
> *The Lord God drowned them all.*

Taken literally, Genesis must be a formidable problem to anyone who believes Genesis to be the inspired Word of God. How does one reconcile faith in an omnipotent, all-knowing, benevolent God, with the God of Genesis? There is a simple solution. Instead of understanding Genesis literally as an accurate description of history, one can see Genesis as a compilation of stories written in ancient times. The authors of Genesis and Gilgamesh were trying to answer troubling questions. Why was life so difficult? Why were there terrible storms and disastrous floods? Were they to blame? Had they offended God? If so, what could they do to get back in God's good graces?

The answers of Genesis are those of our ancestors with scant knowledge of geology, biology, anthropology, or climatology. It is a book written by men, struggling, as we do, to make sense of our existence.

CHAPTER 15

Intelligent Design Vs Evolution

I recently heard a video sermon of an American pastor (with a southern accent) mocking evolution. "What do you believe?" he asked his congregation. "The Book of Genesis, that says God created us in his own image, or Charles Darwin who said we all came from gorillas?" He smiled and shook his head, as if amazed at the incredulity of it. His audience tittered. Holding his black leather bible up for all to see he asked, "What are you going to believe—the theories of atheists or the Word of God?"

The pastor either did not know, or chose to ignore the findings of biologists that our closest relative is not a gorilla, but a chimpanzee with whom we share a 98.4% similarity in our genetic codes. He did not mention that or dwell on the remarkable anatomical similarities between a chimp and a human. Nor did he acknowledge that some Christians believe in both evolution and God.

Ever since 1859, when Charles Darwin published, *On the Origin of Species by Means of Natural Selection,* many Christians have denied and attacked the observations and conclusions of Darwin. They disagree with Darwin's contention that all living things (plants, insects, animals, and humans) have evolved from earlier common ancestors. He called it *descent with modification.* Darwin used the term n*atural selection* to describe the mechanism by which all the modifications occurred.

What is so disturbing to many Christians is that *descent with modification* and the mechanism of n*atural selection* leave out God.

When biologists, biochemists, geneticists and geologists explain the design, complexity and diversity of life, they make no reference to a divine creator or divine intervention. They ignore Genesis as having any scientific credibility. These omissions are very threatening to religious people such as the pastor just mentioned. In order to counter evolution, creationists are now turning to science to validate their faith that life is only possible because of divine intervention. They have two main arguments—the Goldilocks Zone and Intelligent Design.

According to the Goldilocks Zone argument, for life to exist we need a single sun of a particular mass. The earth must have a specific orbit, so that it is not too far away or too close to the sun. We need a specific axial tilt varying between 22.1° and 23.5°. We need a satellite moon to stabilize our orbit and to regulate the ebb and flow of tides. We need an atmosphere that can maintain life, and protect us from the ultra violet rays of the sun. In other words, for life to exist on our planet many laws of science have to be "just right", and this, say the creationists, could not have happened by chance. It shows a divine Creator making conditions just right for our existence.

But is our planet the only one that meets all these conditions? In 1929, Edwin Hubble made the observation that wherever we look, distant galaxies are moving at incredible speeds away from us. He concluded, correctly, that we live in an expanding universe. Astronomers now estimate that our Milky Way Galaxy contains at least 200 billion stars and countless planets in orbit around these stars! Thanks to the 1990 launch of the Hubble telescope, we know there are thousands of other distant galaxies. For ten days astronomers, using the Hubble telescope, focussed the lens on the light from one tiny, black spot in the universe; in that one area, they discovered 3,000 galaxies in what is now called the Hubble Deep Field.

In 2009, NASA launched the Kepler Space Observatory into earth's orbit. It detects extra-solar planets by measuring the dimming of light from a star whenever a planet passes in front of it. Based on data from the Kepler space telescope, astronomers estimated that 17% of the planets in the Milky Way Galaxy are similar in size to our planet. After further analysis of the Kepler data, NASA announced on February 1, 2011, that as many as 54 planets could be habitable. In an April 2011 documentary, Stephen Hawking announced that it is quite reasonable to assume that intelligent life exists elsewhere in this amazingly huge universe. On April

18, 2013, the journal *Science* announced the new discovery of two planet that are "just right" for life. According to William Borucki, the chief scientist of NASA's Kepler telescope, these planets, called Kepler-62-e and Kepler-62-f, meet all the criteria for life to exist!

Thanks to the Hubble telescope and NASA, it no longer makes sense to assume that earth's "Goldilocks Zone" is unique.

The second popular argument that creationists use to refute evolution, is that life is too complex to have come into being through *natural selection*, and *descent with modification*. They contend that the design and complexity of the natural world, and indeed the entire cosmos is incredibly complex. Consequently, they infer that this did not happen by chance, that there is a supreme Designer and Creator, and that there is meaning and purpose behind our existence.

This argument, known as *Intelligent Design,* is not a new one. It has its roots in the teleological arguments of Greek philosophers such as Aristotle and Plato, who saw the "footprints" of God, the creator, in nature and astronomy. So did theologians such as Thomas Aquinas. So did the mathematician and astronomer Isaac Newton (1642-1727). Awed by the complexity and orderliness of the orbits of the planets in our solar system, Newton concluded that an Intelligent Creator was responsible for nudging the planets into their precise orbits.

In the next century, an English theologian, William Paley (1743–1805), refined the "Watchmaker's Analogy". In his book *Natural Theology* of 1802, he argued that if he stumbled upon a pocket watch lying in a heath, he could reasonably assume that it did not just happen to come into being by accident. The watch was too complex, too precise. Someone must have made it and that someone, argued Paley, was God. He extended this argument to the natural world. Paley believed God had meticulously designed *even the most humble and insignificant organisms,* such as the wings and antennae of earwigs.

David Hume (1711-76), Scottish philosopher and historian, pointed out the most obvious flaw in the watchmaker's analogy. If our complex world/cosmos requires a special designer, then who designed the designer? Notwithstanding Hume's unanswerable question, many people continue to believe, as did Paley, that God is the omniscient, intelligent designer.

Scientists, however, are continually finding flaws of design. Why does the laryngeal nerve in mammals take a circuitous route to go from the brain to the larynx? In humans, this nerve originates in the brain, travels down one side of the neck, around the heart and then up the neck to the larynx. In the case of giraffes, the laryngeal nerve takes a circuitous route of 15 feet rather than a direct route of a few inches! Why would an Intelligent Designer allow this unnecessary detour?

To biologists (the exception would be the few who believe in the creation stories of Genesis) the laryngeal nerve is another example of the evolutionary process. Fish evolved before reptiles and mammals. In fish the laryngeal nerve has a direct route from the brain, past the heart to the gills. As fish evolved from reptiles to mammals, the location of the heart changed and necks became necessary—necks which varied in length among species. In other words from a biological perspective, the length and location of the laryngeal nerve is understood as an evolutionary process, and not as a supernatural design.

There are also other physiological human features besides the laryngeal nerve that could benefit from a more intelligent design. For example, for eons people have suffered from arthritic knees and backs. Middle-aged men often make regular nightly trips to the washroom because their urethras run through the centre of the prostate gland—a gland that, unfortunately, enlarges with age.

When we examine the female reproductive system, we find that the pelvic girdle (specifically the hips and birth canal) is responsible for many difficult and lengthy child births. Female hips are narrower than quadrupeds, due to many millennia of walking upright. Bladder and vaginal infections can easily occur due to the proximity to the rectum. Consequently, in third world countries the high mortality rate for mothers and infants is a sad reality. Why are there so many childhood cancers and diseases such as measles, chickenpox, rheumatic fever, whooping cough, scarlet fever and mumps? Why would an omnipotent God create such abnormalities? Could not an Intelligent Designer have given children a stronger, more effective immune system?

Why would an Intelligent Designer create a weather system for our planet that includes lightning, tornadoes, hurricanes, mudslides and floods? Climatic changes have created numerous ice ages in earth's history. The last ice age peaked about 20,000 years ago when glaciers covered large parts of North America and Europe. It caused traumatic changes for all life forms in its path or vicinity. We now know that all these aforementioned weather conditions follow laws of natural science, but did these laws come about as a result of the evolution of our planet, or by the willful design of a Creator? If it is the latter, then an Intelligent Designer is responsible for the climatic disasters that cause so much suffering and death.

The Psalmist looked in awe at the star-studded sky, and concluded that the heavens proclaimed the glory of God. While I too appreciate the beauty and complexity of the heavens, I know that the universe with its exploding suns, black holes, and gamma rays can be a very dangerous place. There are meteorites and asteroids continuously hurtling through space like loose cannonballs on a ship. At the end of the Jurassic Era, a huge meteorite struck the tip of the Yucatan peninsula in Mexico leaving a crater 100 miles wide and 30 miles deep. The impact sent a gigantic tsunami over thousands of miles that devastated life on land and in the sea. The aftermath was even more catastrophic—forest fires and a deadly smothering cloud of ash that blotted out the sun for two years and caused the extinction of countless species. How does one reconcile this disaster with a finely-tuned universe?

If there is an Intelligent Designer responsible for all of creation, why is it that 98 to 99% of all the myriad species that have ever lived are now extinct? The 1909 Burgess Shale discovery in British Columbia provides us with a fossil record of thousands of life forms that perished over 500 million years ago in the Middle Cambrian Period. Another massive extinction ended the Permian Period 250,000,000 years ago. In this latter catastrophe nearly 90% of marine species and 70% of terrestrial species perished. One explanation for this extinction is that a major climatic change occurred. We also have evidence of extensive volcanic action in Siberia that set coal fields ablaze. The resulting ash clouds could have caused massive damage to land and marine life. How does one reconcile these mass extinctions with an intelligent designer?

Why did an Intelligent Designer create reptilian species to dominate the world for over 100 million years? The Jurassic Period featured two kinds of dinosaurs—the hunted and the hunters, the herbivores and the carnivores. It is hard to imagine the carnage and suffering caused by meat-eating dinosaurs such as Tyrannosaurus Rex. Why would a Creator create such pitiless monsters?

We need not, however, go back to the Jurassic Period to discuss violence and suffering in nature. Every year over a million wildebeest, zebras and Thomson gazelles make an arduous and dangerous migration of 500 miles through the Serengeti Conservation Park. These magnificent animals run a gauntlet of lions, hyenas, cheetahs, and crocodiles to reach their new grazing grounds. Apart from those eaten by predators, many drown or perish from exhaustion, hunger, and thirst.

If this "dark side of nature" does not call into question Intelligent Design, at the very least, it makes us stop and wonder about the benevolence of a Creator who has made nature "red in tooth and claw", to quote Alfred Lord Tennyson. William Blake raised the same question in his poetry.

> *Tiger! Tiger! Burning bright,*
> *In the forest of the night;*
> *What immortal hand or eye*
> *Could frame thy fearful symmetry?*

> *When the stars threw down their spears,*
> *And water'd heaven with their tears:*
> *Did he smile his work to see?*
> *Did he who made the lamb, make thee?*

What kind of Creator would allow the malevolent designs we find in nature? Professor William Dembski of the Discovery Institute wrote a book to answer this question. It is called *The End of Christianity: Finding a Good God in an Evil World* (2009). He theorized that the "Fall of Adam" was **retroactively** responsible for all the evil in the world. The effects of the "sin of Adam" went backwards in time. This is Dembski's explanation of the carnage revealed in the fossil records of the Jurassic Period. Amazing! A professor with PhDs in Mathematics and Philosophy, and a M.Div. from Princeton, accepts the theology of the Book of Genesis!

In the 1990's, Michael Behe added his support to proponents of *Intelligent Design*. As a Professor of Biochemistry, Behe argued that certain biochemical structures were "irreducibly complex". In other words their complexity could only have occurred through divine intervention. It is an argument based on what we do not know—a weak point because scientists are continually explaining the "unexplainable".

Behe and Dembski use science subjectively—only when they can use "science" to support one of their theological beliefs. Both of these scientists have been major contributors to the Discovery Institute in Seattle, Washington. Since its founding in 1990, this institute has lobbied school boards, politicians and parents, trying to convince them that *Intelligent Design* should be taught in public high schools as a scientific theory alongside that of evolution. The textbooks they have advocated are anti-evolution and contain creationist perspectives. The courts have ruled against the Institute declaring that its goals and teachings were religious and philosophical—not scientific.

In 2005, a federal court ruled that the Discovery Institute pursues *demonstrably religious, cultural, and legal missions, and the institute's manifesto, the Wedge strategy, describes a religious goal: to reverse the stifling dominance of the materialist worldview, and to replace it with a science consonant with Christian and theistic convictions.* It was the Federal Court's opinion that Intelligent Design was merely a redressing of Creationism, and not a scientific proposition.

It is interesting to note that although Behr has been teaching biochemistry at Lehigh University since 1985, Lehigh University has the following disclaimer on its website.

> *While we respect Prof. Behe's right to express his views, they are his alone and are in no way endorsed by the department. It is our collective position that intelligent design has no basis in science, has not been tested experimentally and should not be regarded as scientific.*

Supporters of Intelligent Design contend that our schools should be fair, and give equal time to teach Intelligent Design as an alternate theory of creation to that of evolution. To that end they are now directing their arguments to politicians, school boards and parents. They have given up trying to convince the scientific community that their views deserve equal status to that of evolution. The following scientific organizations explicitly reject Intelligent Design.

- The American Association for the Advancement of Science (serving 262 affiliated societies and academies of science).
- The American Association of University Professors
- The American Chemical Society (159,000 chemists & chemical engineers).

- The American Geophysical Union (43,000 Earth and space scientists).
- The American Society of Agronomy (10,000 members).
- The American Society for Biochemistry and Molecular Biology (12,000 biochemists and molecular biologists).
- The Federation of American Societies for Experimental Biology (representing 22 professional societies and 84,000 scientists).
- The National Association of Biology Teachers
- The National Center for Science Education
- The National Science Teachers Association (a professional association of 55,000 science teachers and administrators).
- The United States National Academy of Sciences.
- The American Astronomical Society (In 2005 this society's president, Dr. Robert Kirshner, sent this note to President George W. Bush. *Intelligent Design isn't even part of science—it is a religious idea that doesn't have a place in the science curriculum.*)
- The Royal Astronomical Society of Canada. "The RASC Ottawa Centre, then, is unequivocal in its support of contemporary evolutionary theory that has its roots in the seminal work of Charles Darwin and has been refined by findings accumulated over 140 years. Some dissenters from this position are proponents of non-scientific explanations of the nature of the universe. These may include 'creation science', 'creationism', 'intelligent design' or other non-scientific 'alternatives to evolution'".

CHAPTER 16

Ethics Without the Supernatural

In his 2012 Christmas Eve Mass, Pope Benedict XVI pointed out that many people live their lives without making any room for God. He said, *We are so 'full' of ourselves that there is no room left for God. And that means there is no room for others either, for children, for the poor, for the stranger.* The last comment is one I have heard before. To some it seems inconceivable that those who have no room for God would care for others—that they would have a social conscience encompassing not only family and friends, but also strangers.

In this chapter I will examine some of the ethical guidelines of people of faith who made room for God. In the second part of this chapter, I will highlight some of the deeds of people who acted virtuously, not because of any divine commandment, or divine rewards in the hereafter, but because it was the right thing to do.

When I began my first year of university headed for the ministry, I believed that the Bible was a divine moral compass, a foundation for ethics. If someone had asked me for an example from the Bible, I might have said, "The Ten Commandments." I believed, as I had been taught, that these commandments had been given by God to Moses on Mount Sinai. I never questioned these rules. I should have. I should have taken a close, analytical look at these famous commandments found in Exodus 20:3-7.

You shall have no other gods before me. You shall not make yourself a graven image, or any likeness of anything that is in heaven above, or that is in the earth beneath, or that is in the water under the earth; you shall not bow down to them or serve them; for I the Lord your God am a jealous God, visiting the iniquity of the fathers upon the children to the third and fourth generation of those who hate me, but showing steadfast love to thousands of those who love me and keep my commandments. You shall not take the name of the Lord your god in vain; for the Lord will not hold him guiltless who takes his name in vain.

These first three commandments are about the supremacy of an all-powerful, watchful, and jealous God. Those who fail to acknowledge his supremacy will incur his anger. They will be punished, and so will their children, and other innumerable, future, innocent descendants. It is irrational. I, a mere mortal, would never punish my grandchildren for a sin committed by their parents. Nor would you.

The fourth commandment exhorts us to keep the Sabbath in order to remember that God rested on the seventh day of creation.

Remember the Sabbath day, to keep it holy. Six days you shall labor, and do all your work; but the seventh day is a Sabbath to the Lord your God; in it you shall not do any work, you or your son, or your daughter, your manservant, or your maidservant . . .

As with the preceding commandments, there were severe consequences for Jews who broke the Sabbath law.

Moses assembled all the congregation of the people of Israel, and said unto them . . . Six days shall work be done, but on the seventh day you shall have a holy Sabbath of solemn rest to the Lord; whoever does any work on it **shall be put to death;** *and you shall kindle no fire in all your habitations on the Sabbath day.* (Exodus 35:1-3)

Apart from the threat of death, and the injunction not to light a fireplace even on a cold, miserable day, this commandment to rest on the Sabbath makes good sense, because people need to rest. To force people to work seven days a week is folly and heartless. Bodies and minds work better and last longer when people can rest and recharge their batteries.

Actually, many societies have improved upon this commandment. The average working person in Canada and the United States now has two-and-a half days off per week plus four to six weeks of vacation!

Commandment #5 urges us to *Honor your father and your mother, that your days may be long in the land which the Lord your God gives you.* Did you notice the motive here? Don't honor them because they love you and have worked and sacrificed to feed, protect, and clothe you. Don't honor them because they have helped you to find a vocation in life. Don't honour them because they have celebrated your birthdays, your achievements, and your marriage(s). Don't honor them because they have encouraged and supported you even through your temper tantrums and adolescent misadventures. Don't honor them because they have babysat your permissive kids. Honor them so you can live a long life. Humm.

Commandment #6 states, *You shall not kill.* This has a logical, civil ring to it but, it was not meant as a universal law. It did not apply to "the Lord God of Israel" or the Levite priests. When Moses descended from Mount Sinai with the two tablets of stone on which were written the Ten Commandments, he found some of the Israelites were worshipping a golden calf. Moses was enraged.

> *Thus says the Lord God of Israel, 'Put every man his sword on his side, and go to and fro from gate to gate throughout the camp, and slay every man his brother, and every man his companion and every man his neighbour.' And the sons of Levi did according to the word of Moses; and there fell of the people that day about three thousand men.* (Exodus 32:27, 28)

You shall not kill. Moses' sanction did not apply to a sorceress—a female magician who makes false prophesies or who casts evil spells. *You shall not permit a sorceress to live. (See Exodus 22:18 or Leviticus 20:27).* As an aside, these verses were quoted in the Salem trials against "witches".

You shall not kill. It did not apply to the Israelites when they entered the promised land of Canaan, and occupied the territory of the Amorites, the Canaanites, the Hittites, the Perizzites, the Hivites, and the Jebusites (Exodus 34:11). *So Joshua defeated the whole land, the hill country and the Negeb and the lowland and the slopes, and all their kings; he left none remaining, but utterly destroyed all that breathed, as the Lord God of Israel commanded* (Joshua 10: 40). There is no archaeological proof that this happened, but if it did, then it was genocide under the guise of religion.

Commandment #7. *You shall not commit adultery.* It sounds straight forward, as long as we remember that in the Book of Exodus men could have a second wife, concubines, and female slaves. A father could also sell his daughter as a slave (Exodus 21:7-11). Not a great era for women.

Commandment #8. *You shall not steal.* The consequences for theft were severe. If you stole your neighbor's ox and were caught, you were to return five oxen to your neighbor. If you failed to make restitution, then you could be sold into slavery (Exodus 22:1-4).

Commandment #9. *You shall not bear false witness against your neighbour.* To do otherwise perverts justice. A sound injunction.

Commandment #10. *You shall not covet your neighbor's house; you shall not covet your neighbor's wife, or his manservant or his maidservant, or his ox, or his ass, or anything that is your neighbor's.* Wives and servants are listed as possessions along with homes and livestock! Fast forward and apply this injunction to the 21st century. You shall not be envious of any possessions of your neighbor—his trophy wife, his new Mercedes, his beautiful, green, manicured lawn, his original Monet painting, or his well-mannered, successful children. This commandment ranks right up there with a "Mission Impossible" episode.

To summarize, the first four commandments are about the supremacy of God, and the importance of keeping the Sabbath as a day of rest and worship. They form a setting of awe and fear for the six rules that follow. These six commandments forbid us from dishonouring our parents, or committing murder, adultery, theft, perjury, and envy. I am somewhat embarrassed to admit that I once actually believed that these commandments were given to Moses by God on tablets of stone.

The Ten Commandments say nothing about the protection of children, the rights of women, or the abuse of wives and slaves. There is no positive inspiration here for acts of kindness, forgiveness, and generosity to others. Later, when the nomadic Jews occupied Canaan (roughly the area we now call Palestine), they needed a more comprehensive code of behaviour to cover religious and community life in villages and cities. Consequently, their male religious leaders drew up a more extensive code. To give authority to this code, they claimed that all the ordinances came from God. If you are interested in the ethics reflected in their expanded code, try reading the Old Testament Book of Leviticus. Some of the laws will astound you.

For example in Leviticus Chapter 11, we find a list of "unclean" animals, fish, and insects that "are an abomination" to the Lord and which must not be eaten. The list includes pigs, and anything in the sea lacking fins and scales.[34] Chapter 15 deals with unclean "discharges" from the body, including the emission of semen and the menstrual cycle of a woman. Chapter 19:27 forbids a man from trimming his hair or his beard. Chapter 21 forbids those with blemishes or deformities from coming close to the altar of the Lord, so as not to "profane" the sanctuary. Chapter 24 has the oft quoted verse of *an eye for an eye and a tooth for a tooth*. This chapter also calls for the death of anyone who blasphemes the name of the Lord—*and they brought him who had cursed out of the camp, and stoned him with stones (v.22)*. Chapter 25:44-46 gives instructions regarding the buying and bequeathing of male and female slaves.

By quoting only these examples, I realize I am not being fair to the ethics of later books of the Old Testament, such as the Book of Isaiah, written c.5th century BCE. Isaiah's call for righteousness included social justice, such as feeding the hungry, providing for the homeless, and clothing the naked (58:6-7). The prophet Micah also challenged his generation (and ours) when he wrote, *He has showed you, O man what is good; and what does the Lord require of you but to do justice, and to love kindness, and to walk humbly with your God? (6:8)* But justice needs to be spelled out. So does kindness. So does humility. These important principles need to be defined in pragmatic detail. I will return to this point shortly.

Some of you may be wondering why I am not extolling the New Testament as a moral compass. Clearly, the New Testament has many commendable ethical principles such as: *So whatever you wish that men would do to you, do so to them; for this is the law and the prophets* (Matthew 7:12). Jesus showed exemplary concern for the sick and the poor. He had something memorable to say about commandments, as reported in John 13:34: *A new commandment I give to you, that you love one another; even as I have loved you, that you also love one another.* So yes, I can find exemplary ethical principles in the New Testament, provided that I cherry pick, and leave out the irrational parts. Yes, there

---

[34]   If God detested these animals, why did he make them in the first place?

are irrational parts. Consider for example the following words of Jesus found in Matthew 10:34-37.

> *Do not think that I have come to bring peace on earth; I have not come to bring peace, but a sword. For I have come to set a man against his father, and a daughter against her mother . . . He who loves father or mother more than me is not worthy of me; and he who loves son or daughter more than me is not worthy of me . . .*

I wonder how many priests and pastors have ever preached a sermon based on these verses. But more importantly, I wonder how many in their congregations could say that they love Jesus more than their mates, or their parents, or their children?

In Matthew 5:38, 39 Jesus said, *You have heard that it was said 'An eye for an eye and a tooth for a tooth.' But I say to you, do not resist one who is evil. But if any one strikes you on the right cheek, turn to him the other also.* On a personal note, I cannot think of one family member or one friend, who takes these words literally. Thinking internationally, I cannot imagine what would have happened in 1939 if we had followed these words of Jesus when Hitler invaded Poland, or in 1941 when the Japanese bombed Pearl Harbour?

One day when the Apostle Thomas questioned Jesus, Jesus replied with these words: *I am the way, and the truth, and the life; no one comes to the Father, but by me* (John 14:6). It is too bad doubting Thomas did not question Jesus further on the exclusiveness of this claim. He might have asked about the millions of children and adults, past and present, who had no opportunities to learn about Jesus? What would happen to them?

The Apostle Paul, raised in Judaic orthodoxy, had this to say about the women in the congregations of the churches to whom he wrote.[35]

> *. . . the women should keep silence in the churches. For they are not permitted to speak, but should be subordinate, as even the law says. If there is anything they desire to know, let them ask their husbands at home. For it is shameful for a woman to speak in church.* In his letter to Timothy (I Tim. 2:9-11) Paul

---

[35]   1 Corinthians 14:34, 35.

expanded on his views about Christian women. *Women should adorn themselves modestly and sensibly in seemly apparel, not with braided hair or gold or pearly or costly attire but by good deeds, as befits women who profess religion. Let a woman learn in silence with all submissiveness. I permit no woman to teach or to have authority over men; she is to keep silent. For Adam was formed first, then Eve; and Adam was not deceived, but the woman was deceived and became a transgressor.*

In my five years as an ordained minister, I never used these verses as the basis for a single sermon. Nor did I ever choose them as scripture readings in services of worship. I ignored these passages, not because I was happily married and wished to remain so. I ignored these verses because Paul was wrong. If somehow I could go back in time and talk with the apostle, this is what I would like to say to Paul.

The story in Genesis of Eve tempted by a serpent in the Garden of Eden is a myth, and not a very good one. In this story Eve ate of the apple of the knowledge of good and evil, and then persuaded Adam to do the same. Before they ate the fruit, they did not know the meaning of good or evil. So how can you call them disobedient sinners? How could they be disobedient if they did not understand the difference between right and wrong? Yet in this story they are condemned and punished forever. That is very unjust Paul. But what really irks me is that this myth puts the onus of blame on Eve for the Fall (the sin) of humanity. It is a story with very negative and troublesome implications for women.

I realize Paul that you have been taught by your elders and rabbis to believe that women are inferior to men. The truth is that women are inferior to men only in size and strength. That is all. They are just as talented and intelligent as males. When given the opportunity, they can succeed as teachers, law makers, judges, carpenters, and doctors. Women have great leadership skills. This will shock you, but in time, many Christians will accept women as their spiritual leaders. Women will preach. Women will perform marriages, baptisms, and funerals. Women will provide counselling for women and men. In some churches women will administer the Sacrament of Holy Communion. Paul, if you

> *continue to endorse the myth of Adam and Eve, you will help to set in motion a vilification and disparagement of women that will last for centuries.*

I doubt that anything I said would have changed Paul's patriarchal attitude about women. What I have tried to point out in this chapter, is that the bible is inconsistent and unreliable in providing a rational basis for ethics. There are too many passages of scripture that do not make sense, or that jar our innate sense of what is right and wrong. I have quoted only a few of these passages. I have also pointed out that there are laudable ethical principles in the bible, such as those of justice, mercy, love, honesty, and social responsibility for the sick and poor. Such principles are also found in other religions and, as I shall point out shortly, in literature. The challenge is how best to incorporate these principles into the civil and criminal laws of society.

It is obvious that in western countries we no longer grant religious leaders the authority to make and implement our laws. That "experiment" was tried in the Middle Ages with disastrous results. In chapter 12 I listed some of the immoral papal decrees that the Church implemented. I pointed out that during the Inquisition people lost their property, were imprisoned, tortured, and put to death for the "sin" of heresy. Popes gave the rulers of Spain and Portugal "divine" authority to conquer and colonize the New World. Pope Paul IV issued a decree that segregated Jews into ghettos in Italian cities such as Rome.

In medieval times the Church dictated to kings and courts what was right or wrong. If rulers went against the Church, they risked excommunication and an afterlife in heaven. Christians had no opportunity to debate the decrees that came from church councils, popes, and bishops. Nor did most people have the opportunity to study for themselves the creeds or church laws because they were written in Greek or Latin. People were kept in the dark.

William Tyndale was a scholarly, English priest educated at Oxford and proficient in many languages, including French, German, Latin, Hebrew and Greek. In 1535 he was arrested, convicted of heresy and imprisoned for a year. In 1536 he was strangled to death and then burned at the stake. Why? Because he had the audacity, in defiance of church orders, to translate the New Testament into the language of the common people, English. What Tyndale did was right, but, unfortunately, he did so in the wrong place and in the wrong era.

It is little wonder, then, that civil and criminal laws became the responsibility of the state at the municipal, provincial, and federal levels. It is the state that is now socially responsible for the sick, the elderly, the poor, the unemployed, and the disadvantaged. In Ontario, where I live, justice is spelled out in the Ontario Human Rights Code, and in the Canadian Charter of Rights and Freedoms. What is "right" or "wrong" is determined, not by religious leaders, but by our councils, parliaments, and judicial courts. I know we sometimes shake our heads in frustration and disbelief at the raucous, rude behaviour of some of our politicians but, by and large, after the din subsides, reason and flexibility usually prevail. And no one dies. I am being unfair to politicians. In their individual offices, most work conscientiously helping their constituents to find solutions to their problems. On the other hand they are not above the law. Reporters and journalists are ready and willing to expose corruption and abuse of power on the part of our elected officials.

Human beings can act decently and responsibly—as did the Good Samaritan in the Gospel According to Luke, chapter 10:29-37. It is a great parable. One day a lawyer asked Jesus, "Who is my neighbour?" Jesus replied by telling a story. A man travelling to Jericho was set upon by robbers who beat him and left him by the roadside stripped of his clothing and half dead. A Levite, a member of a Jewish tribe responsible for determining the laws of the land, saw the beaten traveller, but walked by! Then a priest saw the poor man by the wayside, but he too did nothing. Lastly, a Samaritan came along. (They were despised by many Jews in this era.) What did he do? He had compassion. He attended to his wounds. He put him on his own donkey and took him to a nearby inn. He stayed for the night caring for the injured man. In the morning he paid the innkeeper saying, *Take care of him; and whatever more you spend I will repay you when I come back.*

To put this parable in a modern context, I run the risk of offending someone, but hopefully, everyone will know I am generalizing, as did Jesus. The first person who walked by the beaten traveller was a lawmaker, maybe a lawyer or a politician. The second person who ignored the beaten traveller was someone who should have know better, who should have been a shining example of compassion. Perhaps he was a bishop or an evangelist. Lastly, the Samaritan who stopped to help could have been either a parolee or an atheist.

I like this parable. It is true that some people selfishly ignore those in need, but there are many who will stop to help those in need. It is part of being human. In the aftermath of 9/11, all the bridges and tunnels in Manhattan were closed for fear that these vulnerable routes might have been rigged with explosives. Half a million people were stranded, unable to get home to their anxious and worried families. The word went out on radio and television that these people were marooned without shelter, warmth, or food. Almost immediately the boats began to arrive—a few ferries, and then a plethora of smaller powerboats and sailboats. In nine hours half a million people were transported from Manhattan to the mainland. It was the largest evacuation in human history—bigger than the 1940 evacuation of Allied troops at Dunkirk. What happened at the docks of Manhattan is a poignant reminder that we are all capable of spontaneous acts of sacrifice and kindness. Ethics in action.

You will recall that on the morning of 9/11, all airports and airways over the continental United States were closed to commercial air traffic. Pilots were advised to land as soon as possible at the nearest airport. As a result 53 commercial airplanes landed at Gander, Newfoundland. The people of Gander, with a population of 14,400, were about to host 10,500 passengers. One of the planes was Delta 15. After waiting all night on the tarmac, 218 exhausted and worried passengers boarded school buses. After clearing Immigration and Customs, they were driven to the town of Lewisporte. The elderly were taken to private homes, and the rest to the local high school, where the students had been enlisted to help. Cots, sleeping bags and mattresses were set up in the gyms. Nearby residents brought in food. Others came with their cars to take people to restaurants or to show them the surrounding area. Some locals organized boat excursions and hikes. Free laundry tokens were distributed.

When the passengers of Delta 15 finally returned to their plane after two days at Lewisporte, they shared their amazing stories of hospitality. On the flight home, the crew and passengers decided to express their gratitude by setting up a college scholarship trust fund for the high school students of Lewisporte. Contributions came from many other individuals, as well as the Delta Corporation. Ten years after 9:11, the trust fund was worth $1.5 million, and had assisted 134 graduating students. In spite of all the bad events we read daily in our newspapers, we need to keep in mind that there are still a lot of good people in the world, people willing to help strangers in times of need.

As a high school English teacher, one of my most rewarding experiences was to teach Harper Lee's novel, *To Kill a Mockingbird.* The story takes place in Maycomb, Alabama and is told from a child's point of view. The little girl, Scout, is proud of Atticus, her father, for ignoring the criticism of family and neighbours in order to defend a black man accused of raping a white woman. Even though Atticus does his best to help the jury of white folk to sift through all the evidence, they find the defendant, Tom Robinson, guilty. Before Atticus can appeal the decision, Tom is shot 17 times by his guards who claim he was trying to escape. Scout is horrified and bewildered at these events. But more danger is ahead for Scout and her brother Jem. Bob Ewell, an abusive alcoholic and the main accuser of Tom Robinson, tries to murder Scout and Jem. A shy and reclusive neighbour, Boo Radley, saves the children. It is a powerful story that has helped many students (and adults) to gain new insights into intolerance and racism, fairness and justice, good and evil, understanding and compassion.

Another of my favourite books is *Catcher in the Rye* by J. D. Salinger. The narrator is a young man, Holden Caulfield. At times, he is rebellious, angry and disillusioned. As he struggles to find meaning in life, he has a recurring dream. It is more like a nightmare. He is the only adult in this huge field of rye in which hundreds of children are running around blissfully unaware that there is a dangerous cliff on one side of the field. Holden frantically tries to protect the children, catching them as they are about to fall over the cliff. He is "the catcher in the rye." The dream helps him find his purpose. Young people can identify with this beautiful story, and Holden's anguished search for meaning in his life.

Like Holden Caulfield, most people want to make a difference, not for any future rewards, but because it's the right thing to do. If we need motivation we might reflect on the Homo sapiens journey that began on the east coast of Africa over 100,000 years ago.[36] It is almost impossible

---

[36] From fossil records, anthropologists estimate that Homo erectus first came out of Africa about 1.8 million years ago. You can research this migration, as well as that of Homo sapiens, from the website of the Smithsonian *National Museum of Natural History.*

to imagine the hardships and sacrifices that our ancestors made for their families and communities. To quote Albert Einstein,

A hundred times every day I remind myself that my inner and outer life depend on the labors of other men, living and dead, and that I must exert myself in order to give in the same measure as I have received and am still receiving.

My saga, *"Faith of Our Fathers" Under the Microscope of Reason and Faith* is almost finished. I hope what I have written has motivated you to examine your own faith, and to arrive at your own conclusions. I have added a short epilogue at the request of one of my friends who reviewed my first draft. She thought readers would be interested in my concluding thoughts and, in particular, in what I now believe. This I have done in the epilogue.

EPILOGUE

I realize that I have been very critical of the Bible. In particular, I have examined many of the inconsistencies and contradictions in the New Testament. By doing so, I have tried to counter the view that the gospels are historical, eyewitness accounts of the life and ministry of Jesus. In my scrutiny of the resurrection of Christ, I have given you a perspective that you may not have considered; namely, that there are valid reasons for either discounting this cardinal Christian belief, or in understanding it spiritually, not physically.

I have been critical of the Christian Church. The writers of the four New Testament gospels deliberately deceived their readers by implying in their titles that their gospels were those of the first disciples—eyewitnesses. I've drawn your attention to the thousands of discrepancies and errors committed by incompetent and careless scribes. Some scribes wilfully added or deleted textual material. I have showed the intolerance of Christian leaders who ordered the banning and burning of manuscripts of those with whom they disagreed. I am skeptical of those who believe Jesus passed on his authority to the Apostle Peter, who in turn passed the mantle of leadership to the succeeding bishop(s) of Rome. This divisive claim ignores the historical evidence that in the first 200 years the most influential Christian leaders were not the bishops of Rome, but the bishops and theologians of Alexandria, Egypt. In these early centuries there were four important centres of Christianity besides Rome; namely, Alexandria, Antioch, Jerusalem, and Constantinople.

In 312 CE, Constantine I, the emperor of the Roman Empire, converted to Christianity, and in the following year legalized Christian worship. From that point onwards, the bishops of Rome were more outspoken in their claim to be the divinely-appointed leaders of the Christian Church. As "Vicars of Christ" some popes made mind-boggling, political decisions. In chapter 12, I named some of the popes responsible for instigating wars, for colonising and exploiting the New World, and for persecuting Jews and heretics. In the examples I cited, I have shown that popes are as prone to sins and errors, as the strutting evangelists, who also claim to speak for God.

I have criticized conservative Christians who would rather believe the ancient stories of Genesis, than the research and findings of biologists, anthropologists, physicists, and astronomers. I find it incredible that in this age of technology and science many people in North America reject evolution, and want their children to be taught that God created the entire cosmos between 6,000 and 10,000 years ago.

When I began collating my notes for this book four years ago, I was an agnostic. By that, I mean I was open to evidence that there was a caring, omnipotent God. In my four years of reading and writing to complete this book, I found no evidence in the Bible, church history, my science research, or the daily headlines of our newspapers, to convince me that there is a caring, omnipotent God—in charge of everything. Thus, in writing *"Faith of Our Fathers" Under the Microscope of Reason and History,* I have made a journey from agnosticism to atheism.

I am comfortable with my perspective, even though I know some will be disappointed that I lost "the Faith of Our Fathers." It would be reassuring to believe that there is a loving, omnipresent God who hears our prayers, and who cares for each of the seven billion people on our planet, plus the billions who preceded us since our ancestors left Africa. But I don't. It would be exonerating (for God) to believe that Satan and his hordes of demons and evil spirits were responsible for much of the evil in the world. But I don't. It would be heartening to believe that there was a divine purpose behind the natural disasters of the world, as well as the insidious bacteria, viruses and cancers that have plagued humanity for eons. But I don't. It would be comforting to believe that there is life after death, that I will be reunited with my loved ones. But I don't.

What do I believe? I can't give you a creed, because I don't have one. Instead, I will mention four virtues to which I aspire. As did the Apostle Paul, I value love[37] as the most important virtue. Next on the pedestal,

---

[37]   I like how Paul defines love in 1 Corinthians 13.

just below that of love, I place knowledge and reason. I would like to think that this book is a testament to my pursuit of those two virtues.

The last virtue may surprise you, but when you have thought about it, you might appreciate my point. I greatly value a deep sense of gratitude.

- I am grateful for the opportunities, past and present, to be a positive influence in the lives of others.
- I am grateful for having been born on this incredible planet into a family with loving, responsible parents and talented, caring siblings.
- I am grateful for my wife and children, grandchildren and great grandchildren. They have enriched my life with their lives and love.
- I am grateful for the friends who have brightened our lives as we travelled together in the journey of life.
- I am grateful to mentors who have inspired me to question and to think—Professor Dobbie, Carl Sagan, Carl Rogers, Bart Ehrman, Mark Twain, and Joseph Campbell.
- I am grateful to those who have used their intelligence and compassion to make our world a better and safer place. Here are a few names that the whole world should remember with heartfelt gratitude.
- Madam and Pierre Curie for discovering radium, and using it to alleviate disease and suffering.
- Dr. Salk for giving us a vaccine that protects our children from the crippling effects of the poliovirus.
- Alexander Fleming for penicillin, an antibiotic that has saved the lives of millions.
- Dr Frederick Banting and Charles Best for discovering insulin to help those suffering from diabetes.
- Louis Pasteur for protecting millions of people through pasteurization and vaccination.
- Gertrude Elion. After her grandfather died of cancer, she decided that no one should suffer such a lingering death. She dedicated your life to biochemical research, and helped discover drugs to combat leukemia, gout, malaria, septicemia and herpes.

- Dr. Nevin S. Scrimshaw. His medical professors were disappointed when he decided to focus his time and talents on nutrition. Little did they realize that millions of lives would benefit from the affordable foods he created for infants and children in third-world countries.
- *Doctors Without Borders.* Since 1971 they have gone to over 80 countries to provide medical aid, hope, and reconciliation to victims of civil wars and natural disasters.

These are only a few of the many benefactors of the human race. They have helped to conquer humanity's most ancient scourges, not by sermons, prayers and prophecies, but by science and a deeply held resolve to help their fellow man. I would like to conclude by sharing two quotations with you. The first is from Bertrand Russell (1872-1970), a British philosopher, mathematician, and social critic.

> *Three passions, simple but overwhelmingly strong have governed my life: the longing for love, the search for knowledge, and unbearable pity for the suffering of mankind.*

The second is from Joseph Campbell (1904-1987), an American Professor at Sarah Lawrence College in the city of Yonkers, New York. He was raised as a Roman Catholic, but through his study of comparative religions and the mythologies of numerous cultures, past and present, he lost the faith he once held. This loss did not lead to despair. He saw life as a journey and an adventure.

> *People say that what we're all seeking is a meaning in life. I don't think that's what we're really seeking . . . what we're seeking is an experience of being alive, so that our life experiences on the purely physical plane will have resonances within our own innermost being and reality, so that we actually feel the rapture of being alive.*

ADDENDUM A

Early Christian Authors (100 to 400 CE)

Justin Martyr (100 to 165 CE) of Samaria (Jordan)

Martyr was a Platonist philosopher before he converted to Christianity. He wrote extensively defending Christian doctrines against pagan and Gnostic teachings. His writings included "Apology to the Christian Religion" (c.155 CE), and "Dialogue with Trypho the Jew" (c.160 CE). To prove that Jesus was fully human **and** fully divine, Justin quoted over 300 times from the Old Testament and almost 100 times from apocryphal literature (texts that dealt with the end of days). It is important to note that in his defence of Christianity, he did not use excerpts from the New Testament gospels. This omission supports the research of New Testament scholars, such as Bart Ehrman and John Dominic Crossan, that the four New Testament gospels were written decades after the life of Jesus (c. 70 to 95 CE), and had not yet reached Justin Martyr in Samaria.

Justin also debated with Trypho over the nature of the Messiah. Trypho, a Jew, expected a Messiah who would free Israel from the yoke of Roman rule, and restore the glory and might of Israel to the days of Kings Solomon and David. In contrast, Justin Martyr taught that Jesus, through his suffering on the cross, had fulfilled the vision of Isaiah that the long-awaited saviour would be a suffering Messiah. Trypho disagreed. He found it incredulous that Jesus, a lowly son of a carpenter, crucified by the Romans, could be the Messiah.

Martyr saw the crucifixion in a different light. He stated that God would punish those responsible for the murder of the Messiah, Jesus. Martyr saw the destruction of the Temple of Jerusalem in 70 CE as a clear sign of God's displeasure! He predicted that more punishment would follow. He even claimed that circumcision had been preordained by God, so that Jews could be identified and punished!

Marcion (100 to 160 CE) of Pontus, an Ancient Part of Asia Minor (now Turkey)

Marcion was a Christian Gnostic. Unfortunately, none of his writings have survived. We know very little about the man, but we do know a good deal about his theology through Iranaeus and Tertullian who detailed and criticized Marcion's writings. As a Gnostic, Marcion taught that knowledge did not come solely through scripture or the teachings of church leaders. He believed that spiritual knowledge also came through personal experience and intuition. He taught that a spiritual person could be open to a continuing revelation, and consequently, possess special knowledge of what to believe and how to live.

His views on scripture also caused dissension. While his Christian peers revered the Old Testament for prophesying the coming of the Messiah, Jesus, Marcion rejected the Old Testament as being sacred. He saw the God of the Old Testament as a vengeful lawgiver. To clarify what was sacred, Marcion chose a canon of 11 texts from the numerous texts and gospels then in existence. His canon consisted only of the Gospel of Luke and ten epistles of Paul. He achieved consensus, by a committee of one.

He was convinced, however, that these 11 texts had been corrupted. False believers had added or deleted verses according to their own beliefs. To "correct" these unscrupulous scribes, he revised his entire canon taking out all references to the Old Testament God, and any references to Jewish Law as tenets Christians had to follow! I wonder if he saw the irony in what he did. It is hardly surprising that by 144 CE a number of church leaders had branded Marcion a heretic, and ordered the destruction of all his writings.

Iranaeus (c.120 to 200 CE) the Bishop of Lyons, France

Iranaeus was raised in a Christian family in Smyrna of Asia Minor (now Izmir, Turkey). He wrote numerous Apologies in his opposition to Gnosticism. One of his major works, "Against Heresies", consisted of five volumes. He also listed Christian manuscripts he deemed to be sacred. To the 11 sacred texts chosen by Marcion, he added the Gospels of Matthew, Mark and John. His rationale in doing so is bizarre. He wrote, *It is not possible that the gospels can be either more or fewer in number than they are. For since there are four zones of the world in which we live, and four principal winds . . . it is fitting that she should have four pillars.*[38]

Bishop Iranaeus is the only early Christian writer on record to declare that Jesus was at least 50 when he was crucified—not 30. To believe otherwise, he warned, was heresy!

Tertullian (c. 160 to 220 CE)

Tertullian was born in Carthage, North Africa (Tunisia). Called "the Father of Latin Christianity", Tertullian strongly opposed Gnostics, especially their claim that Jesus only "appeared" to be human. He wrote a five-volume work "Against Marcion". He too believed that the Roman destruction of Jerusalem in 70 C.E. was an act of God, a punishment because the Jews had rejected and crucified their Messiah. He is the first known Christian to use the term "Trinity" (Latin *trinitas*) describing God as three persons, yet one substance. This concept was refined by the church councils of 325 and 381, so that by the end of the fourth century, there was an established doctrine of the Trinity; namely, the deity of the Father, Son, and Holy Spirit under one Godhead, in three co-equal and co-eternal Persons.

In later life, Tertullian became a Montanist, believing in a direct, ecstatic, personal experience of the Holy Spirit. It is a little ironic that in this Monastic perspective, he shared a similar spiritualism found in Gnosticism. Although never labelled a heretic, Tertullian's Montanistic views were not widely accepted.

---

[38]   See *Against Heresies* 3.111.7.

Clement of Alexandria, Egypt (c.150 to 215 CE)

Clement was a theologian, as well as a scholar of Greek philosophy and pagan literature. He was the head of the Catechetical School of Alexandria. He used contemporary philosophies and traditions to support and clarify Christian tenets. In one of his writings, *The Stromata*, Clement endorsed the doctrine of apocatastasis, the belief that all people will eventually be saved. He viewed the punishments of God as saving and disciplinary, and thus necessary for conversion.

Clement was familiar with Gnosticism. He described Basilides, a Gnostic theologian, as one devoted to the contemplation of divine things. Influenced perhaps by his familiarity with Gnostic literature, Clement taught that through faith one attains a higher state of knowledge, a "knowing" that leads to goodness and virtue. As did many Gnostics, he believed that scripture should be understood as myth and allegory, and not interpreted literally. Although esteemed as one of the early Church Fathers, his liberal interpretation of scripture was clearly at odds with the orthodox views that eventually prevailed at the Council of Nicaea in 325 CE.

Origen (c. 185 to 254 CE) of Alexandria, Egypt

Origen was a student of Clement. He too thought that scripture should be understood allegorically. He taught that a literal approach, while preferred by the uneducated, was irrational. According to Origen, a literal interpretation of the crucifixion was a doctrine "fit only for children". He wrote that it was heretical to interpret the Bible literally.[39]

Although Origen only made specific references to the Gospel of Matthew, he was aware of other gospels. In his work *Against Celsus (6:36)*, he corrects Celsus for mocking Jesus "as a mere carpenter". *Celsus is blind also to this, that in none of the Gospels current in the Churches is Jesus himself ever described as being a carpenter.* This is an interesting comment because in Mark 6:3 we read, *Is not this (Jesus) the carpenter, the son of Mary* . . . If Origen is right, then someone erred in copying and translating later editions of Mark's gospel.

---

[39]   *On First Principles*, Book 3, Chapter 3, v.1)

Like Justin Martyr and Tertullian, Origen was harsh in his condemnation of Jews for rejecting Jesus as the Messiah. He wrote, *It was right that the city in which Jesus underwent such sufferings should be completely destroyed, and that the Jewish nation should be over thrown.*[40]

Eventually, Origen and his writings were condemned. The church councils of 400, 543 and 553 declared his teachings to be heretical. Christians who read his books could be excommunicated.

Eusebius (260 to 340 CE) Bishop of Caesarea (Now in Jordan)

Eusebius is famous or infamous for several reasons. Instead of following the allegorical and symbolic approach of Christian theologians like Origen and Clement, he believed that scripture should be accepted and understood as literal, historical truths. He was the first early Christian leader to write a history of the Church. In his "Ecclesiastical History" he undertook the task of recording the first 300 years of Christianity. Consequently, he was regarded for many centuries as the Father of Church History. Today, his reputation as a historian is seriously maligned by many scholars. Charles B. Waite in his *History of the Christian Religion* had this to say about Eusebius.

> *No one has contributed more to Christian history, and no one is guilty of more errors . . . the statements of this historian are made, not only carelessly and blunderingly, but in many instances in falsification of the facts of history. Not only the most unblushing falsehood, but literary forgeries of the vilest character darken the pages of his . . . writings.*

Edward Gibbon, the author of "The Decline and Fall of the Roman Empire", was equally scathing in his criticism. He accused Eusebius of having no literary pangs of conscience in relating whatever would glorify the church, and in suppressing whatever would be critical of the church. Other authorities who concur with Gibbon include Alexander Wilder, Gerald Massey, G.R.S. Mead, John Lawrence von Mosheim, J.M. Robertson, Paul Harper and Bart Ehrman.

---

[40] *Against Celsus* 4.22.

ADDENDUM B

Christian Texts From 1516-1881

Printed Texts. The Gutenberg press revolutionized the reproduction of scripture making Bibles much more accessible and affordable, especially for the general public. The first printed bible came out in 1452. Over the next 60 years, many bibles were printed. They varied significantly one from the other depending on the translation skills of the editor, and the manuscripts he chose. Some editors chose literal translations while others selected translations that best conveyed the meaning of the text. Following are the three most important printed editions. These are the templates for today's New Testaments.

(1) Novum Testamentum was printed in 1516, thanks to the efforts of D. Erasmus (1466-1536), a classical Dutch scholar. It was a formidable task. By the time he was born, 5,700 Greek manuscripts had been discovered, as well as 10,000 manuscripts of the Latin Vulgate! As you can see from the following quotation, he was strongly motivated.

> *But one thing the facts cry out, and it can be clear, as they say, even to a blind man, that often through the translator's clumsiness or inattention the Greek has been wrongly rendered; often the true and genuine reading has been corrupted by ignorant*

> *scribes, which we see happen every day, or altered by scribes who are half-taught and half-asleep.*[41]

His edition is famous for the controversy caused by his initial exclusion of one verse of scripture—1 John 5:8. Much to the consternation of a few peers, in his first two editions, Erasmus did not include this "Trinity" verse known as Comma Johanneum. He excluded it because it was not found in the 12th century Greek manuscripts he was using. (Author's note: nor is this controversial verse found in three of the earliest manuscripts; namely, Vaticanus, Sinaiticus or Alexandrinus.) When his critics found a Greek manuscript that included the verse, Erasmus reluctantly included the "Trinity" verse in the third edition of Novum Testamentum. Some scholars think his critics used a fifth century manuscript that had the disputed verses as a gloss—words added in the margin that eventually were added to the body of a 1520 Greek manuscript.

You must by now be curious to read this disputed verse. Here it is, as found in the Authorized King James Version of the Bible. *For there are three that bear record in heaven, the Father, the Word, and the Holy Ghost: and these three are one.* In their debates over the doctrine of the Trinity, none of the early Church Fathers used this verse—a clear indication that they had never seen it. Most modern translations omit this verse in its entirety, including the New Vulgate. To read more of the debate you can research the following sources: *Erasmus and the Comma Johanneum* by H. J. de Jonge in 1980 p.385, and also *A History of the Debate Over 1 John 5:7,8* by Michael Maynard, p. 383.

(2) Textus Receptus. There were five editions of Erasmus' Novum Testamentum, with the last one coming out in 1535. These editions were the first of a succession of printed Greek texts that became known as Textus Receptus. Robert Estienne (1503-1559) printed four editions of the New Testament. He was the first editor to print the Bible in numbered verses. The brothers Bonaventure and Abraham Elzevir printed a 1624 Greek edition of the New Testament. In their preface they were the first to use the term "Textus Receptus". Thus, Textus Receptus (with Erasmus as the main contributor) became the precursor of many

---

[41] Epistle 337 from *The Collected Works of Erasmus* Vol. 3, p.134.

subsequent Bibles such as the German Lutheran Bible, the English Tyndale Bible, The Geneva Bible and the King James Version.

(3) The New Testament in the Original Greek. The next important edition of the New Testament was published in 1881—*The New Testament in the Original Greek*. It is a monumental work by two Cambridge classical scholars, Wescott and Hort. Their goal was to identify and remove textual errors, so that their New Testament would be as close as possible to the original manuscripts. Wescott and Hort relied heavily on the two earliest manuscripts, Sinaiticus and Vaticanus. As well, their research included early scriptural fragments, Codices Bezae and Alexandrinus, old Latin texts including Jerome's Vulgate Bible, early Syriac texts, and later medieval manuscripts. It took them 28 years of arduous analysis to produce their edition of the New Testament! Biblical scholars today, with few exceptions, applaud the procedures they followed, and the many source texts they researched.

Although some scholars criticize Wescott and Hort for placing too much emphasis on the fourth century manuscripts of Codex Sinaiticus and Codex Vaticanus, their edition is seen by most textual scholars as a marked improvement over Textus Receptus. Their edition became the basis for many subsequent bibles. I use the words "most textual scholars" because the Greek Orthodox Church decided that other codices were more reliable. Their New Testament editions are based mainly on Codex Alexandrinus (400-440 CE), as well as a number of ninth century texts (based on a text type called Byzantine).

In the past 100 years there have been many discoveries of early fragments and manuscripts. With modern technology (including computer programmes), today's scholars have new tools for reading, examining and dating old and fragile scripts. New editions of the New Testament will continue to be printed.

ADDENDUM C

11 of the 95 Theses of Martin Luther

Martin Luther introduced his famous letter with these words. "Out of love and concern for the truth, and with the object of eliciting it, the following heads will be the subject of a public discussion at Wittenberg under the presidency of the reverend father, Martin Luther, Augustinian, Master of Arts and Sacred Theology, and duly appointed Lecturer on these subjects in that place. He requests that whoever cannot be present personally to debate the matter orally will do so in absence in writing."

8. *The penitential canons apply only to men who are still alive, and, according to the canons themselves, none applies to the dead.*

11. *It is a wrongful act, due to ignorance, when priests retain the canonical penalties on the dead in purgatory.*

20. *Therefore the pope, in speaking of the plenary remission of all penalties, does not mean "all" in the strict sense, but only those imposed by himself.*

21. *Therefore those preachers of indulgences are in error who say that by the pope's indulgences a man is freed from every penalty, and saved.*

25. *The power which the pope has, in a general way, over purgatory, is just like the power which any bishop or curate has, in a special way, within his own diocese or parish.*

27. *There is no divine authority for preaching that the soul flies out of the purgatory immediately the money clinks in the bottom of the chest.*

33. *Men must be on their guard against those who say that the pope's pardons are that inestimable gift of God by which man is reconciled to Him.*

43. *Christians should be taught that one who gives to the poor, or lends to the needy, does a better action than if he purchases indulgences.*

53. *They are enemies of Christ and of the pope, who bid the Word of God be altogether silent in some Churches, in order that pardons may be preached in others.*

79. *To say that the cross, emblazoned with the papal arms, which is set up [by the preachers of indulgences], is of equal worth with the Cross of Christ, is blasphemy.*

86. *Why does not the pope, whose wealth is today greater than the riches of the richest, build just this one church of St. Peter with his own money, rather than with the money of poor believers?*

Addendum D

The Eastern Crusades

Historical Background.

In 380 CE, Christianity became the official state religion of the Roman Empire by the Edict of Thessalonica. The Roman emperors responsible for passing this important law were Theodosius I, Gratian, and Valentinian II. I thought you might be interested in the warnings and tone of the last two sentences of this edict.

> *We authorize the followers of this law to assume the title of Catholic Christians; but as for the others, since, in our judgment they are foolish madmen, we decree that they shall be branded with the ignominious name of heretics, and not presume to give to their conventicles[42] the name of churches. They will suffer in the first place the chastisement of the divine condemnation and in the second the punishment of our authority which in accordance with the will of Heaven we shall decide to inflict. (Codex Theodosianus, xvi.1.2.)*

Once Christianity was officially recognized, the new religion spread rapidly, and interest in visiting the Holy Lands was widespread. Over the next 300 years, many Christians from Europe made a sacred pilgrimage

---

[42]   A small unofficial meeting of lay people

to see such sites as Nazareth and Jerusalem. It was an arduous journey, but doable until the seventh century.

In 610, Mohammed began his mission as a prophet of Allah, and founded a new religion, Islam. Within a century of Mohammed's death, all the regions from Egypt to Turkey had been invaded and conquered by Islamic armies. It was a Jihad, a religious war waged against infidels—those who refused to believe in the revelations that Mohammed had received from Allah, through the Angel Gabriel.

Christians in the conquered countries were given three choices. They could accept Islam, or pay a toll-tax (Jizyah) by which, as unbelievers, they would be protected. Their third option was death as sanctioned in the Quran 9:5. *Fight and slay the Pagans wherever ye find them.* Needlessly to say, the expansion of Islam was swift and dramatic. In the first three centuries of Islam, thousands of Christians were forced at the point of a sword to convert or be slain. Hundreds of churches were destroyed or desecrated. Many European pilgrims were denied access to the Holy Land.

In 1095, European Christians were well aware of what had happened in the Holy Land, and to Christian Centres at Antioch, Acre, Ephesus and Alexandria. The Old Roman Empire, with Constantinople as its Capital, had been reduced to little more than the area of Greece. In desperation, the Emperor Alexios Komnenos, appealed to Pope Urban II to help free their eastern brothers and sisters in Christ from Islamic rule.

The First Crusade (1095-1100).

In 1095, Pope Urban II (1035-1099) gave an impassioned speech at the Council of Clermont calling for a holy war to liberate the eastern churches. We have no transcript of what he said, only five versions written years afterwards. In these accounts, Urban is reputed to have said that all who died by land or sea or in battle against the Muslims would have remission of their sins and the assurance of an eternity in the kingdom of heaven. We do have, however, a letter that he sent to the Crusaders in 1095. Here, in part, is what he wrote.

Urban, bishop, servant of the servants of God, to all the faithful, both princes and subjects, waiting in Flanders; greeting, apostolic grace, and blessing . . . Your brotherhood, we believe, has long since learned from many accounts that a barbaric fury has deplorably afflicted and laid waste the churches of God in the regions of the Orient. More than this, blasphemous to say, it has even grasped in intolerable servitude its churches and the Holy City of Christ, glorified by His passion and resurrection. Grieving with pious concern at this calamity, we visited the regions of Gaul and devoted ourselves largely to urging the princes of the land and their subjects to free the churches of the East. We solemnly enjoined upon them at the council of Auvergne such an undertaking, as a preparation for the remission of all their sins. (C. Krey, *The First Crusade: The Accounts of Eyewitnesses and Participants*, Princeton: p. 42-43).

This call to arms was heeded. Early in the summer of 1096, a German army of 10,000 began the long march. Militarily, the First Crusade was a success. In 1099, after capturing and looting Antioch, the Crusaders captured Jerusalem. There are conflicting reports of what happened to the defenders and residents of Jerusalem. It is likely that in the slaughter that followed, a few Muslim and Jewish residents were spared. Before leaving for Germany, the Crusaders established five states, each with a garrison and a Christian governing body.

The Second Crusade (1145-47).

After Islamic forces retook Edessa (one of the Crusader States), Pope Eugene III issued the bull *Quantum Praedecessores*. It called for a holy war and offered the same indulgences promised to participants of the First Crusade (remission of sins and a hereafter in heaven). Led by the Kings of France and Germany, the separate armies began their overland journey. As with the first campaign, the armies (to the dismay of the pope) ruthlessly attacked Jewish communities, looting and killing. After an unsuccessful siege of Damascus, the armies returned home without accomplishing their goals.

Ronald V. Evans

The Third Crusade (1189-1192).

This is the most famous Crusade. It is called "The Kings Campaign" with the three principal leaders being King Richard I of England, Philip II of France, and Frederick I, the German Holy Roman Emperor. Thanks to five Hollywood films, we saw epic battle scenes of carnage, chivalry and courage. In the 1954 movie, *King Richard and the Crusades,* King Richard, the "Coeur de Lion", leads gallant templar knights in full armour mounted on splendid steeds. His opponent, Saladin, is a formidable enemy leading an army of thousands of archers and mounted warriors.

Although the campaign was heralded as a great victory, Jerusalem was not recaptured. Instead of waging a lengthy and costly siege of Jerusalem, Richard signed a treaty with Saladin. Under the treaty terms, Jerusalem would remain under Muslim control, but unarmed Christian pilgrims and merchants could safely enter the city. The treaty did not bring stability or peace to the Holy Lands. In only ten years another Crusade was undertaken.

The Fourth Crusade (1202-1204).

Pope Innocent III pleaded for a campaign to liberate the Holy Land from Muslim domination. Mindful of what might happen, he explicitly banned attacks on Christian states. The Crusading armies ignored this directive. Instead of sailing to Egypt to begin their Crusade, they sailed from Venice to attack and sack the Croatian port city of Zara, a Greek Orthodox community. From Zara they sailed to Constantinople, the Capital of the Eastern Roman Empire. Following a successful siege, many of the inhabitants were slaughtered. Religious icons were either stolen or melted down for their silver and gold. Churches and cathedrals were desecrated.

When Pope Innocent III learned of the attacks and atrocities, he sent a scathing letter of rebuke to the Crusaders, excommunicating them all and ordering them to keep their sacred vow to free the Holy Land. But the leaders and armies, now short on resolve and energy, returned to their homelands. This Crusade was over. The Pope, however, was not averse to accepting some of the stolen loot that arrived for Rome—sacred icons, jewels, gold and silver. So it is not surprising that he softened his stance and allowed the crusaders back into the Church.

The Fifth Crusade (1213-1231).

In 1213, Pope Innocent III called for yet another Holy War. Considering the previous failures and losses, his call to battle was unpopular even with the accompanying offers of indulgences. It was not until 1217 that Oliver of Cologne and William I of Holland gathered men and supplies and sailed for Egypt. They successfully besieged, captured and looted the Egyptian city of Damietta, before marching towards Cairo. It was the time of year when the Nile River floods. Trapped by the floods and weakened by military losses, the army surrendered, and Damietta was returned to Islamic control. It was the end of the Fifth Crusade—a humiliating disaster.

The Sixth Crusade (1228-1229).

Just prior to his coronation in 1220, as Emperor of the Holy Roman Empire, Frederick II made a vow to Pope Honorius III to organize and lead the sixth Crusade. It was not until 1227, however, that Frederick, with a formidable German army, set sail from Southern Italy to begin the expedition. After only three days, he turned back due to an epidemic affecting many of his soldiers. Pope Gregory IX viewed this decision as yet another example of reluctance and procrastination. He excommunicated Frederick for failing to keep his vow.

The next year, still at odds with the pope, Frederick arrived with his army in Acre, the nominal capital of the Kingdom of Jerusalem. Support from the Christian forces at Acre was divided. Some were reluctant to follow one who lacked papal approval and support; others were wary of Frederick's political goals. Realizing that a military campaign would likely fail, Frederick negotiated a truce with the Muslim sultan, Al-Kamil, who had political problems of his own. Consequently, a treaty was signed in 1229 whereby Frederick regained control of Jerusalem, Nazareth, Bethlehem, and a small coastal strip of land. The Muslims retained control over the al-Aqsa Mosque, the Dome of the Rock, and the Temple area of Jerusalem. There was a further stipulation that the fortifications of Jerusalem were not to be restored.

This ten-year truce was not well received by the pope who had no part to play in either the campaign or the negotiations. The terms were condemned also by some of the Crusaders including the Templar Knights and the Hospitaller Knights. The campaign had ended with a measure of success and virtually no loss of life.

The Seventh Crusade (1248-1250).

After Jerusalem fell to the Turks in 1244, King Louis IX of France was the only European ruler to respond to the pope's plea to liberate Jerusalem. With an army of 15,000 he landed in June of 1249 at Damietta, Egypt. The port city fell with little resistance. Due to the annual flooding of the Nile, he waited six months before advancing towards Cairo. An Egyptian force led by Baibers, the Turkish commander, defeated the French army. Louis then began a futile siege of the Egyptian city of Mansourah. With his army short of supplies, he began the march back to Damietta only to be met by another Egyptian army. The French army was annihilated and Louis captured. It took a ransom of 800,000 gold coins to secure his release. Another humiliating defeat.

The Eighth Crusade (1270).

Alarmed by new military conquests of Christian territories by Baibars (the Turkish commander), Louis IX of France once again raised an army. In July of 1270, he landed in Tunisia to begin the siege of Tunis. His plan was to use Tunis as a base from which to attack Egypt. Due to the heat and poor drinking water, many soldiers became sick, including Louis IX. With his death the siege ended, and his brother Charles negotiated a peace agreement with the Sultan, Baibars. This last Crusade lasted one year. Only one Christian outpost remained in the Middle East—that of Acre.

Author's Note.

You may have noticed that I have not described the "**Children's Crusade**". That is because there is no credible evidence that it ever happened—even though the notion of a Children's Crusade was recounted as history for centuries. How did this happen?

In 1212/13 there were two bands of wandering people in northern France and Germany. It is likely that these roving groups were poor, displaced people. They were sometimes referred to, condescendingly, as *pueri*. In Latin, it meant young boys, but it also had a colloquial meaning of young men of low social standing. A mistranslation of the term *pueri* may be the simplest explanation for the Children's Crusade.

From the middle of the twelfth century until modern times, two tales were embellished for centuries. The first involved Nicholas, a young German shepherd lad with great persuasive powers of speech. He and about 20,000 followers set out from Cologne to cross the Alps to the port city of Genoa. Their mission was to convert the Muslim populations to Christianity. Nicholas promised that upon reaching Genoa, God would part the seas so they could reach the Holy Land. It was a catastrophe as 14,000 died crossing the Alps. When they reached Genoa, they discovered that God had neglected to part the seas. Following the advice of Pope Innocent III, Nicolas tried to return home, but died crossing the Alps. Back home, his father was hung by angry family members who had lost loved ones who had followed Nicholas.

In the second tale, a 12-year-old French shepherd boy, called Stephan of Cloves, claimed to have a letter from Jesus for the King of France—a letter calling for yet another Holy Crusade to be led by Stephan. King Philip II was neither impressed by the letter, nor the reputed 30,000 eager followers, many of whom were *pueri*. Stephan and his group eventually reached Marseille. Disheartened and exhausted, they dispersed and returned home.

By the middle of the 12th century these two tales were well on their way to becoming legends, thanks to imaginative chroniclers who were not present in 1212/13, and who misunderstood the term *pueri*. Modern historians such as Peter Raedts, George Duby and Oswald Russell dismiss these two tales as myth.

Addendum E

Decrees of the Roman Pontiffs

1—Decrees Pertaining to Salvation

Pope Innocent III made the following proclamation in 1215. *"There is but one universal Church of the faithful, outside of which no one at all can be saved"*. In 1302, Pope Boniface VIII issued a bull, called the *Unam Sanctum*. It concludes with these words. *Furthermore, we declare, we proclaim, we define that it is absolutely necessary for salvation that every human creature be subject to the Roman Pontiff.* Pope Eugene IV made an even stronger statement in his *Cantate Domino* bull of 1441.

> *The Holy Roman Church firmly believes, professes and teaches that none of those who are not within the Catholic Church, not only Pagans, but Jews, heretics and schismatics, can ever be partakers of eternal life, but are to go into the eternal fire 'prepared for the devil, and his angels' (Mt. xxv. 41), unless before the close of their lives they shall have entered into that Church;*

The Second Vatican Council, convened by Pope John Paul VI in 1962, acknowledged in chapter two, paragraph 16 of the document, *Lumen Gentium*, that there are Christians outside the Roman Catholic Church.

> *. . . many elements of sanctification and of truth are found outside its visible confines . . . the Church knows that she is joined in many ways to the baptized who are honored by the name of Christ, but who do not however profess the Catholic faith in its entirety or have not preserved unity or communion under the successor of Peter.*

> *The non-Christian may not be blamed for his ignorance of Christ and his Church; salvation is open to him also, if he seeks God sincerely and if he follows the commands of his conscience, for through this means the Holy Ghost acts upon all men; this divine action is not confined within the limited boundaries of the visible Church.*

In the year 2000, Cardinal Ratzinger, as Prefect of the *Congregation for the Doctrine of the Faith,* issued the document, *Dominus Iesus on the unicity and salvific universality of Jesus Christ and the Church.* It stated that although salvation is possible to those who are not Roman Catholics or Eastern Orthodox, the prayers and rituals of other religions may help or hinder their believers. Some practices may prepare their membership to absorb the Gospel; however, those rituals which *depend on superstitions or other errors . . . constitute an obstacle to salvation.* Members of other religions are *gravely deficient* relative to members of the Church of Christ who already have "*the fullness of the means of salvation.*"

3—Decrees Pertaining to Witches

In 1484, Pope Innocent VIII issued the following decree, *Summis Desiderantes Affectibus.*

> *It has come to our ears . . . that many persons of both sexes, unmindful of their own salvation and straying from the Catholic Faith, have abandoned themselves to devils, incubi and succubi, and by their incantations, spells, conjurations, and other accursed charms and crafts, enormities and horrid offences, have slain infants yet in the mother's womb, as also the offspring of cattle,*

have blasted the produce of the earth . . . they hinder men from performing the sexual act and women from conceiving . . .

4—Decrees Pertaining to the Colonization of the New World (1492-1898)

The papal bull of Pope Nicholas V, *Dum Diversas*, issued in 1452, reads as follows.

> We *grant you by these present documents, with our Apostolic Authority, full and free permission to invade, search out, capture, and subjugate the Saracens* (Muslims) *and pagans and any other unbelievers and enemies of Christ wherever they may be, as well as their kingdoms, duchies, counties, principalities, and other property . . . and to reduce their persons into perpetual slavery.*

In 1493, Pope Alexander V issued a bull, *Inter Caetera*. It granted Spain all lands west and south of any of the islands of the Azores or the Cape Verde Islands.

> *Alexander, bishop, servant of the servants of God, to the illustrious sovereigns, our very dear son in Christ, Ferdinand, king, and our very dear daughter in Christ, Isabella, queen of Castile, Leon, Aragon, Sicily, and Granada, health and apostolic benediction. Among other works well pleasing to the Divine Majesty and cherished of our heart, this assuredly ranks highest, that in our times especially the Catholic faith and the Christian religion be exalted and be everywhere increased and spread, that the health of souls be cared for and that barbarous nations be overthrown and brought to the faith itself . . . we . . . give, grant, and assign to you and your heirs and successors . . . all islands and mainlands found and to be found, discovered and to be discovered towards the west and south, by drawing and establishing a line from the Arctic pole, namely the north, to the Antarctic pole, namely the south, no matter whether the said mainlands and islands are found . . . in the direction of India or towards any other quarter, the said line to be distant one hundred leagues*

121

towards the west and south from any of the islands commonly known as the Azores and Cape Verde.

5—Decrees Pertaining to Martin Luther

Pope Leo X issued the bull, *Decet Romanum Pontificemat.* In addition to excommunicating Luther, the pope had this to say in the third and fourth paragraphs of Section III.

> *Our decrees which follow are passed against Martin and others who follow him in the obstinacy of his depraved and damnable purpose, as also against those who defend and protect him with a military bodyguard, and do not fear to support him with their own resources or in any other way, and have and do presume to offer and afford help, counsel and favour toward him. All their names, surnames and rank—however lofty and dazzling their dignity may be—we wish to be taken as included in these decrees with the same effect as if they were individually listed and could be so listed in their publication, which must be furthered with an energy to match their contents.*
>
> *On all these we decree the sentences of excommunication, of anathema, of our perpetual condemnation and interdict; of privation of dignities, honours and property on them and their descendants, and of declared unfitness for such possessions; of the confiscation of their goods and of the crime of treason; and these and the other sentences, censures and punishments which are inflicted by canon law on heretics and are set out in our aforesaid missive, we decree to have fallen on all these men to their damnation.*

6—Decrees Pertaining to Jewish Italian Ghettoes

Following are the first ten decrees of the papal document *Cum Minis Absurdum,* issued by Pope Paul IV in 1555.

1. *We ordain that for the rest of time, in the City as well as in other states, territories and domains of the Church of Rome itself, all Jews are to live in only one [quarter] to which there is only one entrance and from which there is but one exit, and if there is not that capacity [in one such quarter, then], in two or three or however many may be enough; [in any case] they should reside entirely side by side in designated streets and be thoroughly separate from the residences of Christians, [This is to be enforced] by our authority in the City and by that of our representatives in other states, lands and domains noted above.*

2. *Furthermore, in each and every state, territory and domain in which they are living, they will have only one synagogue, in its customary location, and they will construct no other new ones, nor can they own buildings. Furthermore, all of their synagogues, besides the one allowed, are to be destroyed and demolished. And the properties, which they currently own, they must sell to Christians within a period of time to be determined by the magistrates themselves.*

3. *Moreover, concerning the matter that Jews should be recognizable everywhere: [to this end] men must wear a hat, women, indeed, some other evident sign, yellow in color, that must not be concealed or covered by any means, and must be tightly affixed [sewn]; and furthermore, they cannot be absolved or excused from the obligation to wear the hat or other emblem of this type to any extent whatever and under any pretext whatsoever of their rank or prominence or of their ability to tolerate [this] adversity, either by a chamberlain of the Church, clerics of an apostolic court, or their superiors, or by legates of the Holy See or their immediate subordinates.*

4. *Also, they may not have nurses or maids or any other Christian domestic or service by Christian women in wet-nursing or feeding their children.*

5. *They may not work or have work done on Sundays or on other public feast days declared by the Church.*

6. *Nor may they incriminate Christians in any way, or promulgate false or forged agreements.*

7. *And they may not presume in any way to play, eat or fraternize with Christians.*

123

8. *And they cannot use other than Latin or Italian words in short-term account books that they hold with Christians, and, if they should use them, such records would not be binding on Christians.*
9. *Moreover, these Jews are to be limited to the trade of rag-picking . . ., and they cannot trade in grain, barley or any other commodity essential to human welfare.*
10. *And those among them who are physicians, even if summoned and inquired after, cannot attend or take part in the care of Christians.*

7—Decrees Pertaining to Papal Infallibility and the Assumption

The First Vatican Council of 1870 defined papal infallibility as follows: *We teach and define that it is a dogma Divinely revealed that the Roman pontiff when he speaks ex cathedra, that is when in discharge of the office of pastor and doctor of all Christians, by virtue of his supreme Apostolic authority, he defines a doctrine regarding faith or morals to be held by the universal Church, by the Divine assistance promised to him in Blessed Peter, is possessed of that infallibility with which the Divine Redeemer willed that his Church should be endowed in defining doctrine regarding faith or morals, and that therefore such definitions of the Roman pontiff are of themselves and not from the consent of the Church irreformable. So then, should anyone, which God forbid, have the temerity to reject this definition of ours: let him be anathema* (denounced and excommunicated). (Chapter 4 of "Pastor Aeternus")

In 1950, Pope Pius XII produced this papal document, *Munificentissimus Deus. Now God has willed that the Blessed Virgin Mary should be exempted from this general rule. She, by an entirely unique privilege, completely overcame sin by her Immaculate Conception, and as a result she was not subject to the law of remaining in the corruption of the grave, and she did not have to wait until the end of time for the redemption of her body. By the authority of our Lord Jesus Christ, of the Blessed Apostles Peter and Paul, and by our own authority, we pronounce, declare, and define it to be a divinely revealed dogma: that the Immaculate Mother of God, the ever Virgin Mary, having completed the course of her earthly life, was assumed body and soul into heavenly glory.*

8—Decrees Pertaining to Birth Control

In 1968, Pope Paul VI issued his encyclical letter, *Humanae Vitae*. It reads as follows. *Therefore we base our words on the first principles of a human and Christian doctrine of marriage when we are obliged once more to declare that the direct interruption of the generative process already begun and, above all, all direct abortion, even for therapeutic reasons, are to be absolutely excluded as lawful means of regulating the number of children. Equally to be condemned, as the magisterium of the Church has affirmed on many occasions, is direct sterilization, whether of the man or of the woman, whether permanent or temporary. Similarly excluded is any action which either before, at the moment of, or after sexual intercourse, is specifically intended to prevent procreation.*

ADDENDUM F

Geological Clocks

How old is the earth? In 1953 Clair Cameron Patterson, a geochemist, determined that our planet was 4.6 billion years old (plus or minus 70 million years). He based this age on isotopic dating of five meteorites and samples of lead from Pacific deep-sea sediment. Recent studies confirm this dating. According to the U.S. Geological Survey of 1997, the earth is c. 4.5 billion years old. See also *Special Publications, Geological Society of London 190 (1):* 205-221.

How old is the Universe? Astronomers now date the universe as being approximately 13.7 billion years old. To understand how they arrived at this age, google, "Cepheid variable stars".

Fossils and Sedimentary Rocks

Aeons ago, dead plants and life forms were sometimes buried in sediments such as mud, sand or lime. The softer parts rotted but the harder more durable parts remained. With the passage of time the sediment surrounding them hardened into sedimentary rocks, due to the pressure of subsequent layers of sediment and/or the weight of water. Thus, the outlines of these life forms were preserved. We call these outlines fossils, petrified remains of long-dead organisms.

According to Darwin, when we go back millions and millions of years, we discover that life forms become less complicated—simpler.

This is what we find in the fossil records. The earliest fossils are those of bacteria cells, then single-celled organisms, and later, more complex forms of multi-cellular life forms. When we study vertebrate fossils, we see that fish came first, then reptiles, then birds, and lastly, mammals.

William Smith (1769-1839), is renown today as the founding father of English geology. As a surveyor he had an important role in the building of canals throughout England—canals that carried goods such as coal. As these canals were dug, he took careful notice of the different layers of rock and the fossils in the rocks. Over his lifetime, he made meticulous notes and diagrams of sedimentary layers and fossils. He made several logical conclusions. One, if rocks from different sites contain the same fossils, they are from the same era. Two, if some fossils found in lower strata are not found in higher strata, they had become extinct.

To share these important discoveries, he painstakingly drew a beautiful, hand-painted map of what lay beneath the surface of England and Wales. Eight feet high and six feet long, it was indeed a "map that changed the world". I recommend Simon Winchester's *The Map that Changed the World,* published in 2001 in New York by Harper Collins. I think this is a "must read" for young people being schooled in science at home.

Smith's map and notes had profound implications for geology and religion. For example, Smith observed that the oldest fossils found at the lowest strata of sedimentary rock (Pre-Cambrian—earlier than 545 million years ago) contained single-celled marine organisms. The organisms in the Cambrian era (545-495 million years ago) were more complex and multi-celled. In other words organisms became more complex with time. These observations directly contradicted the widely-held belief of Smith's day that life was created in six days, 6,000 years ago.

Using fossils as relative indicators of time, geologists have subdivided the strata into three large-scale blocks of time. The Palaeozoic Period, containing the skeletons of petrified life forms, is dated from 550 to 250 million years ago. The next era, the Mesozoic Period, contained the skeletons of **different** petrified organisms. In other words a major extinction of species had occurred. This era ended 65 million years ago with the extinction of dinosaurs. We are currently in the third geological era, the Cainozoic Period.

From our knowledge of these underlying strata of our planet, we know the earth is very old. It takes **time** to turn sand, lime or mud into solid rock. But how does one date these three blocks of time? How can a scientist determine that one layer of rock is c. 2 billion years old or that the earth is c. 4.55 billion years old? These questions bring us to the second geological clock—radioactive decay.

Radioactive Decay

To understand this geological clock you may need to review the following principles of science as they pertain to elements, light, a spectrometer, magma, uranium and carbon 14.

- All matter is made up of elements. There are over 100 (106 and counting) unique substances such as gold, carbon and hydrogen. These substances cannot be separated into simpler substances. Each element is made from tiny identical particles called atoms.
- Light is made up of little packets of energy called photons. We get colours because each element emits photons at a specific energy. White light is a mixture of a number of photons of different energies. By sending white light through a prism, all the colours it contains are separated out into a spectrum (a rainbow range of colours from ultra-violet to infra-red).
- By using a spectrometer scientists can analyze a spectrum and identify the atoms (elements) that make up the light source because each element has its own spectral fingerprint. Thus astronomers can look at the light from a distant star, split it into its rainbow spectrum with a prism, and determine the elements that make up the star!
- Magma is a mixture of molten rock, solids, and volatiles (chemical elements and compounds with low boiling points such as nitrogen, water and carbon dioxide). Magma is found beneath the surface of the earth and is extremely hot—700 °C to 1300 °C. Elements such as uranium can be found in varying concentrations and sporadically throughout the magma. When magma comes to the surface through earthquakes and volcanic action, the magma cools into igneous rock formations.

- The element uranium is unstable because the nuclei of their atoms are continually releasing energy. This process is called radio-active decay. Two types of particles are emitted. Alpha decay involves emissions of helium nuclei (two protons and two neutrons) and beta decay involves emission of an electron. The discharge of these particles is the cause of the "clicks" in a Geiger counter.

- As uranium 238 decays it changes into different elements—such as protactinium 234, uranium 234, thorium 230, radon 222, polonium 214, bismuth 210, polonium 210, and then with a final alpha decay to lead 206. Uranium undergoes decay at a constant and measurable rate. Thus, the ratio of lead 206 to uranium 238 in a rock sample gives an accurate measure of the age of the rock. The half-life value of uranium 238 to become lead 206 is 4.5 billion years.

- Scientists use a mass spectrometer to measure the ratio of uranium to lead. This method of dating was developed at the University of Chicago by Clair Cameron Patterson. From 1948-1953, he collected rock samples from around the globe. By using a mass spectrograph to measure the ratio of uranium to lead isotopes, he determined that the earth was 4.55 billion years old (plus or minus 70 million years). His work has stood the test of time. His estimate of the age of the earth is still accepted some 60 years later!

Carbon 14

Carbon 14 is another radioactive element used by scientists to determine the age of substances such as trees and bones. Carbon 14 forms when cosmic rays collide with nitrogen atoms in the earth's atmosphere. Some of these radioactive carbon atoms are absorbed into living organisms such as trees. When a tree dies it no longer absorbs carbon 14 atoms; consequently, its carbon 14 begins to undergo radioactive decay at a measurable rate with a half-life of 5,730 years.

Using this knowledge, scientists can take a piece of wood from an ancient tomb, and compare the amount of carbon 14 with the amount of Carbon 14 from a living tree. The ratio provides an accurate measure of the age of the wood in the tomb. Or to simplify the explanation, if carbon from a piece of wood in an ancient burial site contains only half as much carbon14 as carbon 14 from a living tree, the age of the old wood is approximately 5,730 years old.

This method of dating gives a good fix on the age of organic matter but only up to a point. After eight half-lives, only 1/256 of the original radioactive carbon remains, which is too little to make a reliable measurement. This means that this method of carbon-dating is only accurate for objects up to about forty thousand years old.

Since 1977 scientists, however, have used an even more accurate method of carbon 14 dating—mass spectrometry or atomic spectrometry. By this process only a few grams or milligrams of a sample are ionized, accelerated and passed through a magnetic field. Using this process scientists can date samples of wood or bone that are 70,000 years old.

Bibliography

Religion

Acharya S. *Suns of God: Krishna, Buddha and Christ Unveiled.* Kempton, Illinois: Adventures Unlimited Press, 2004.

Campbell, Joseph. *The Power of Myth: with Bill Moyers.* New York: Doubleday, a division of Bantam Doubleday Dell Publishing Group, Inc., 1988.

Crossan, John Dominic. *The Historical Jesus: The Life of a Mediterranean Jewish Peasant.*
New York: HarperCollins, 1991.

Dawkins, Richard. *The God Delusion.* Great Britain: Bantam Press, 2006.

Ehrman, Bart D. *Misquoting Jesus: The Story Behind Who Changed the Bible and Why.* New York: HarperCollins, 2005.

Ehrman, Bart D. *Lost Christianities: The Battle for Scripture and the Faiths We Never Knew.* Oxford: Oxford University Press, 2003.

Ehrman, Bart D. *Jesus, Interrupted: Revealing the Hidden Contradictions in the Bible (and Why We Don't Know About Them).* New York: HarperCollins, 2009.

Ehrman, Bart D. *The Lost Gospel of Judas Iscariot: A New Look at Betrayer and Betrayed.* Oxford: Oxford University Press, 2006.

Ehrman, Bart D. *Lost Scriptures: Books That Did Not Make It into the New Testament.* Oxford: Oxford University Press, 2003.

Harpur, Tom. *The Pagan Christ: Recovering the Lost Light.* Toronto: Thomas Allen Publishers, 2004.

133

Harris, Sam. *The End of Faith: Religion, Terror, and the Future of Reason.* New York: W.H. Norton & Company Ltd., 2004.

Harris, Sam. *Letters to a Christian Nation.* New York: Alfred A. Knopf, a division of Random House, Inc., 2006.

Hitchens, Christopher. G*od Is Not Great: How Religion Poisons Everything.* Toronto: McClelland & Stewart Ltd., 2007.

Kohn, Risa Levitt. *Dead Sea Scrolls: Words that Changed the World.* Beauceville East, Quebec: printed by Transcontinental Interglobe, 2009.

Schweitzer, Albert. *The Quest of the Historical Jesus.* London: A. & C. Black Ltd., 1911.

Twain, Mark. *Letters from the Earth: Uncensored Writings.* New York: HarperCollins Publishers Inc., 1938.

Wright, Robert. *The Evolution of God.* New York: Back Bay Books by Little, Brown and Company, 2009

Science

Gribbon, John, Consultant Editor. *A Brief History of Science.* Lewes, East Sussex: The Ivy Press Limited, 1998.

Sagan, Carl. *The Demon-Haunted World: Science as a Candle in the Dark.* New York: Ballantine Books, a division of Random House Inc., 1996.

Scott, Eugene C. *Evolution Vs Creationism: An Introduction.* Berkeley and Los Angeles, University of California Press, 2004.

Weiner, Jonathan. *The Beak of the Finch: A Story of Evolution in Our Time.* New York: Division Books, a division of Random House, Inc., 1995.

Winchester, Simon. *The Map that Changed the World.* New York: Harper Collins Publishers, 2001.

Edwards Brothers Malloy
Oxnard, CA USA
July 10, 2013